Learning React

Second Edition

The Pearson Addison-Wesley Learning Series

LEARNING
ANGULAR
A Hands-On Guide to Angular 2 and Angular 4
SECOND EDITION
BRAD DAYLEY
BRENDAN DAYLEY
CALEB DAYLEY

SECOND EDITION
LEARNING
Blender
A Hands-On Guide to Creating 3D Animated Characters
OLIVER VILLAR

LEARNING TO
PROGRAM
STEVEN FOOTE

THE LANGUAGE of SQL
SECOND EDITION
LARRY ROCKOFF

Visit **informit.com/learningseries** for a complete list of available publications.

The **Pearson Addison-Wesley Learning Series** is a collection of hands-on programming guides that help you quickly learn a new technology or language so you can apply what you've learned right away.

Each title comes with sample code for the application or applications built in the text. This code is fully annotated and can be reused in your own projects with no strings attached. Many chapters end with a series of exercises to encourage you to reexamine what you have just learned, and to tweak or adjust the code as a way of learning.

Titles in this series take a simple approach: they get you going right away and leave you with the ability to walk off and build your own application and apply the language or technology to whatever you are working on.

Make sure to connect with us!
informit.com/socialconnect

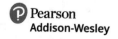

Pearson
Addison-Wesley

informIT.com
the trusted technology learning source

Learning React

Second Edition

Kirupa Chinnathambi

♦ Addison-Wesley

Learning React, Second Edition

ISBN-13: 978-0-13-484355-1
ISBN-10: 0-13-484355-X

Library of Congress Control Number: 2017957370

4   2019

Trademarks

All terms mentioned in this book that are known to be trademarks or service marks have been appropriately capitalized. Pearson cannot attest to the accuracy of this information. Use of a term in this book should not be regarded as affecting the validity of any trademark or service mark.

Warning and Disclaimer

Every effort has been made to make this book as complete and as accurate as possible, but no warranty or fitness is implied. The information provided is on an "as is" basis. The author and the publisher shall have neither liability nor responsibility to any person or entity with respect to any loss or damages arising from the information contained in this book.

Special Sales

For information about buying this title in bulk quantities, or for special sales opportunities (which may include electronic versions; custom cover designs; and content particular to your business, training goals, marketing focus, or branding interests), please contact our corporate sales department at corpsales@pearsoned.com or (800) 382-3419.

For government sales inquiries, please contact governmentsales@pearsoned.com.

For questions about sales outside the U.S., please contact intlcs@pearson.com.

Editor
Mark Taber

Managing Editor
Sandra Schroeder

Project Editor
Mandie Frank

Copy Editor
Krista Hansing

Indexer
Erika Millen

Proofreader
Jeanine Furino

Technical Editor
Trevor McCauley

Editorial Assistant
Vanessa Evans

Designer
Chuti Prasertsith

Compositor
codemantra

Accessing the Free Web Edition

Your purchase of this book in any format includes access to the corresponding Web Edition, which provides several special online-only features:

- The complete text of the book
- Updates and corrections as they become available

The Web Edition can be viewed on all types of computers and mobile devices with any modern web browser that supports HTML5.

To get access to the *Learning React* Web Edition, all you need to do is register this book:

1. Go to www.informit.com/register.
2. Sign in or create a new account.
3. Enter the ISBN: **9780134843551**.
4. Answer the questions as proof of purchase.
5. The Web Edition will appear under the Digital Purchases tab on your Account page. Click the Launch link to access the product.

❖

To my dad!

(Who always believed in me—even if what I was often doing made no sense to him...or to me for that matter! ☺)

❖

Contents at a Glance

Table of Contents

About the Author

Kirupa Chinnathambi has spent most of his life trying to teach others to love web development as much as he does.

In 1999, before *blogging* was even a word, he started posting tutorials on kirupa.com. In the years since then, he has written hundreds of articles, penned a few books (none as good as this one, of course!), and recorded a bunch of videos you can find on YouTube. When he isn't writing or talking about web development, he spends his waking hours helping make the web more awesome as a Program Manager at Microsoft. In his nonwaking hours, he is probably sleeping—or writing about himself in the third person.

You can find him on Twitter (twitter.com/kirupa), Facebook (facebook.com/kirupa), or email (kirupa@kirupa.com). Feel free to contact him anytime.

Acknowledgments

First, none of this would be possible without the support and encouragement of my awesome wife, **Meena**. If she hadn't put her goals on hold to allow me to spend six months designing, writing, and rewriting everything you see here, writing this book would have been a distant dream.

Next, I'd like to thank **my parents** for always encouraging me to aimlessly wander and enjoy free time doing what I like—such as teaching complete strangers via the Internet in the late 1990s how to do cool things with programming. I wouldn't be half the rugged indoorsman/scholar/warrior I am today without them both ☺.

On the publishing side, writing the words you see here is the easy part. Getting the book into your hands is an amazingly complex process. The more I learn about all the moving pieces involved, the more impressed I am with all the individuals who work tirelessly behind the scenes to keep this amazing machinery running. **To everyone at Pearson** who made this possible, thank you! There are a few people I'd like to explicitly call out, though. First, I'd like to thank **Mark Taber** for continuing to give me opportunities to work together, **Chris Zahn** for patiently addressing my numerous questions and concerns, **Krista Hansing** for turning my version of English into something humanly understandable, and **Loretta Yates** for helping make the connections a long time ago that made all of this happen. The technical content of this book has been reviewed in great detail by my long-time friends and online collaborators **Kyle Murray (a.k.a. Krilnon)** and **Trevor McCauley (a.k.a. senocular)**. I can't thank them enough for their thorough (and, frequently, humorous!) feedback.

Introducing React

Ignoring for a moment that web apps today both *look* and *feel* nicer than they did back in the day, something even more fundamental has changed. The way we architect and build web apps is very different now. To highlight this, let's take a look at the app in Figure 1.1.

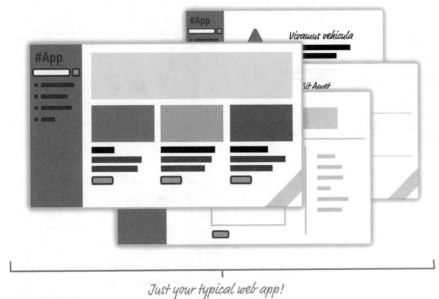

Just your typical web app!

Figure 1.1   An app.

This app is a simple catalog browser for something. As with any app of this sort, you have your usual set of pages revolving around a home page, a search results page, a details page, and so on. In the following sections, let's look at the two approaches we have for building this app. Yes, in some mysterious fashion, this leads to us getting an overview of React as well.

Onward!

Old-School Multipage Design

If you had to build this app a few years ago, you might have taken an approach that involved multiple, individual pages. The flow would have looked something like Figure 1.2.

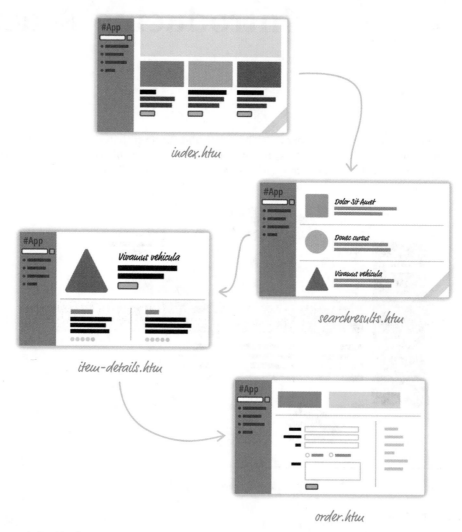

Figure 1.2   Multipage design.

For almost every action that changes what the browser displays, the web app navigates you to a *whole different page*. This is a big deal, beyond just the less-than-stellar user experience users will see as pages get torn down and redrawn. This has a big impact on how you maintain your app state. Except for storing user data via cookies and some server-side mechanism, you simply don't need to care. Life is good.

New-School Single-Page Apps

These days, going with a web app model that requires navigating between individual pages seems dated—really dated. Check out Figure 1.3.

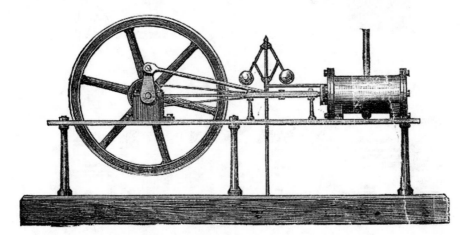

Figure 1.3   The individual page model is a bit dated, like this steam engine.

Instead, modern apps tend to adhere to what is known as a **single-page app (SPA) model**. This model gives you a world in which you never navigate to different pages or ever even reload a page. In this world, the different views of your app are loaded and unloaded into the same page itself.

For our app, this looks something like Figure 1.4.

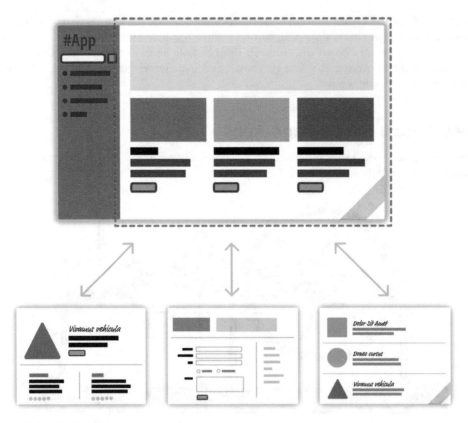

Figure 1.4   Single-page app.

As users interact with our app, we replace the contents of the dotted red region with the data and HTML that matches what the user is trying to do. The end result is a much more fluid experience. You can even use a lot of visual techniques to have your new content transition nicely, just like you might see in cool apps on your mobile device or desktop. This sort of stuff is simply not possible when navigating to different pages.

All of this might sound a bit crazy if you've never heard of single-page apps, but there's a very good chance you've run into some of them in the wild. If you've ever used popular web apps like Gmail, Facebook, Instagram, or Twitter, you've used a single-page app. In all those apps, the content gets dynamically displayed without requiring you to refresh or navigate to a different page.

Now, I'm making these single-page apps seem really complicated. That's not *entirely* the case. Thanks to a lot of great improvements in both JavaScript and a variety of third-party frameworks and libraries, building single-page apps has never been easier. That doesn't mean there's no room for improvement, though.

When building single-page apps,, you'll encounter three major issues at some point:

1. **In a single-page application, you'll spend the bulk of your time keeping your data in sync with your UI.** For example, if a user loads new content, do you explicitly clear out the search field? Do you keep the active tab on a navigation element still visible? Which elements do you keep on the page, and which do you destroy?

   These are all problems that are unique to single-page apps. When navigating between pages in the old model, we assumed everything in our UI would be destroyed and just built back up again. This was never a problem.

2. **Manipulating the DOM is really, really slow.** Manually querying elements, adding children (see Figure 1.5), removing subtrees, and performing other DOM operations is one of the slowest things you can do in your browser. Unfortunately, in a single-page app, you'll be doing a lot of this. Manipulating the DOM is the primary way you are able to react to user actions and display new content.

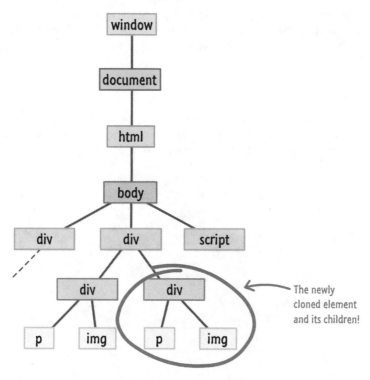

The newly cloned element and its children!

Figure 1.5   Adding children.

3. **Working with HTML templates can be a pain.** Navigation in a single-page app is nothing more than you dealing with fragments of HTML to represent whatever you want to display. These fragments of HTML are often known as **templates**, and using JavaScript to manipulate them and fill them out with data gets really complicated really quickly.

To make things worse, depending on the framework you're using, the way your templates look and interact with data can vary wildly. For example, this is what defining and using a template in Mustache looks like:

```
var view = {
  title: "Joe",
  calc: function() {
    return 2 + 4;
  }
};

var output = Mustache.render("{{title}} spends {{calc}}", view);
```

Sometimes your templates look like clean HTML that you can proudly show off in front of the class. Other times, your templates might be unintelligible, with a boatload of custom tags designed to help map your HTML elements to some data.

Despite these shortcomings, single-page apps aren't going anywhere. They are a part of the present and will fully form the future of how web apps are built. That doesn't mean you have to tolerate these shortcomings, of course. Read on.

Meet React

Facebook (and Instagram) decided that enough is enough. Given their huge experience with single-page apps, they released a library called **React** to not only address these shortcomings, but also change how we think about building single-page apps.

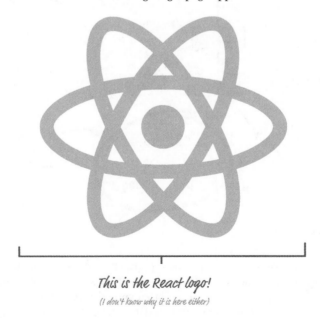

This is the React logo!
(I don't know why it is here either)

In the following sections, we look at the big things React brings to the table.

Automatic UI State Management

With single-page apps, keeping track of your UI and maintaining state is hard … and also very time consuming. With React, you need to worry about only one thing: the final state of your UI. It doesn't matter what state your UI started out in. It doesn't matter what series of steps your users took to change the UI. All that matters is where your UI ended up (see Figure 1.6).

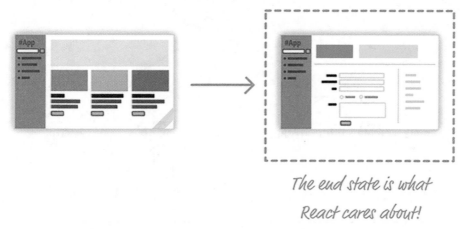

The end state is what React cares about!

Figure 1.6   The final or end state of your UI is what matters in React.

React takes care of everything else. It figures out what needs to happen to ensure that your UI is represented properly so that all that state-management stuff is no longer your concern.

Lightning-Fast DOM Manipulation

Because DOM modifications are really slow, you never modify the DOM directly using React. Instead, you modify an in-memory *virtual* DOM (resembling what you see in Figure 1.7).

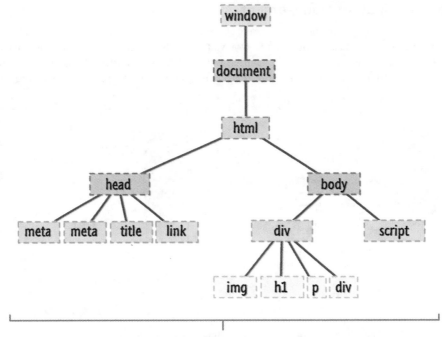

The virtual DOM looks nothing like this. It is also
not going to be this colorful :(

Figure 1.7   Imagine an in-memory virtual DOM that sort of looks like this.

Manipulating this virtual DOM is extremely fast, and React takes care of updating the real DOM when the time is right. It does so by comparing the changes between your virtual DOM and the real DOM, figuring out which changes actually matter, and making the fewest number of DOM changes needed to keep everything up-to-date in a process called **reconciliation**.

APIs to Create Truly Composable UIs

Instead of treating the visual elements in your app as one monolithic chunk, React encourages you to break your visual elements into smaller and smaller components (see Figure 1.8).

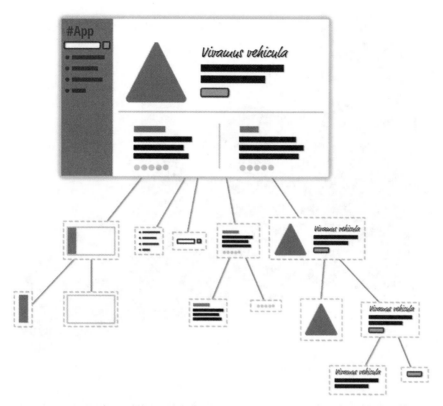

Figure 1.8 An example of how the visuals of your app can be broken into smaller pieces.

As with everything else in programming, it's a good idea to make things modular, compact, and self-contained. React extends that well-worn idea to how we think about user interfaces. Many of React's core APIs revolve around making it easier to create smaller visual components that can later be composed with other visual components to make larger and more complex visual components—kind of like the Russian matryoshka dolls in Figure 1.9. (see Figure 1.8):

Figure 1.9   Russian matryoshka dolls.

This is one of the major ways React simplifies (and changes) how we think about building the visuals for our web apps.

Visuals Defined Entirely in JavaScript

While this sounds ridiculously crazy and outrageous, hear me out. Besides having a really weird syntax, HTML templates have traditionally suffered from another major problem: You are limited in the variety of things you can do inside them, which goes beyond simply displaying data. If you want to choose a piece of UI to display based on a particular condition, for example, you have to write JavaScript somewhere else in your app or use some weird framework-specific templating command to make it work.

For example, here's what a conditional statement inside an EmberJS template looks like:

```
{{#if person}}
  Welcome back, {{person.firstName}} {{person.lastName}}!
{{else}}
  Please log in.
{{/if}}
```

React does something pretty neat. By having your UI defined entirely in JavaScript, you get to use all the rich functionality JavaScript provides for doing all sorts of things inside your templates. You are limited only by what JavaScript supports, not limitations imposed by your templating framework.

Now, when you think of visuals defined entirely in JavaScript, you're probably thinking something horrible that involves quotation marks, escape characters, and a whole lot of `createElement` calls. Don't worry. React allows you to (optionally) specify your visuals using an HTML-like syntax known as **JSX** that lives fully alongside your JavaScript. Instead of writing code to define your UI, you are basically specifying markup:

```
ReactDOM.render(
  <div>
    <h1>Batman</h1>
    <h1>Iron Man</h1>
    <h1>Nicolas Cage</h1>
    <h1>Mega Man</h1>
  </div>,
  destination
);
```

This same code defined in JavaScript would look like this:

```
ReactDOM.render(React.createElement(
  "div",
  null,
  React.createElement(
    "h1",
    null,
    "Batman"
  ),
  React.createElement(
    "h1",
    null,
    "Iron Man"
  ),
  React.createElement(
    "h1",
    null,
    "Nicolas Cage"
  ),
  React.createElement(
    "h1",
    null,
    "Mega Man"
  )
), destination);
```

Yikes! Using JSX, you are able to easily define your visuals using a very familiar syntax, while still getting all the power and flexibility that JavaScript provides.

Best of all, in React, your visuals and JavaScript often live in the same location. You no longer have to jump among multiple files to define the look and behavior of one visual component. This is templating done right.

Just the V in an MVC Architecture

We're almost done here! React is not a full-fledged framework that has an opinion on how everything in your app should behave. Instead, React works primarily in the View layer, where all of its worries and concerns revolve around keeping your visual elements up-to-date. This means you're free to use whatever you want for the M and C parts of your MVC (a.k.a. Model-View-Controller) architecture. This flexibility allows you to pick and choose technologies you are familiar with, and it makes React useful not only for new web apps you create, but also for existing apps you'd like to enhance without removing and refactoring a whole bunch of code.

Conclusion

As new web frameworks and libraries go, React is a runaway success. It not only deals with the most common problems developers face when building single-page apps, but it also throws in a few additional tricks that make building the visuals for your single-page apps *much* easier. Since it came out in 2013, React has also steadily found its way into popular web sites and apps that you probably use. Besides Facebook and Instagram, some notable ones include the BBC, Khan Academy, PayPal, Reddit, *The New York Times*, and Yahoo!, among many others.

This article was an introduction to what React does and why it does it. In subsequent chapters, we'll dive deeper into everything you've seen here and cover the technical details that will help you successfully use React in your own projects. Stick around.

2

Building Your
First React App

Thanks to the previous chapter, you probably now know all about the backstory of React and how it helps even your most complex user interfaces sing. For all the awesomeness that React brings to the table, getting started with it (kind of like this sentence) is not the most straightforward. It has a steep learning curve filled with many small and big hurdles, as in Figure 2.1.

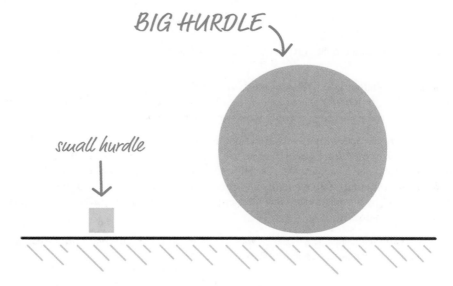

Figure 2.1   Hurdles come in a variety of sizes. Some are big. Some are small.

In this chapter, we start at the very beginning and get our hands dirty by building a simple React app. You'll encounter some of these hurdles head-on, and some of these hurdles you'll skip over—for now. By the end of this chapter, not only will you have built something you can proudly show off to your friends and family, but you'll have set yourself up nicely for diving deeper into all that React offers in future chapters.

Dealing with JSX

Before we start building our app, there's an important point to cover first. React isn't like many JavaScript libraries you might have used. It doesn't get too happy when you simply refer to code you've written for it using a script tag. React is annoyingly special that way, and it has to do with how React apps are built.

As you know, your web apps (and everything else your browser displays) are made up of HTML, CSS, and JavaScript (see Figure 2.2).

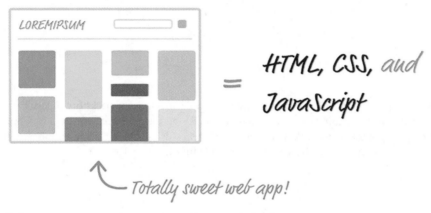

Figure 2.2   Web apps are built in HTML, CSS, and JavaScript.

It doesn't matter whether your web app was written using React or some other library, such as Angular, Knockout, or jQuery. The *end result* has to be some combination of HTML, CSS, and JavaScript; otherwise, your browser really won't know what to do.

Now, here's where the special nature of React comes in. *Besides normal HTML, CSS, and JavaScript, the bulk of your React code will be written in JSX.* As I mentioned in Chapter 1, "Introducing React," JSX is a language that allows you to easily mix JavaScript and HTML-like tags to define user interface (UI) elements and their functionality. That sounds cool and all (and you'll see JSX in action in just a few moments), but there's a slight problem. Your browser has no idea what to do with JSX.

To build a web app using React, we need a way to convert our JSX into plain old JavaScript that your browser can understand (see Figure 2.3).

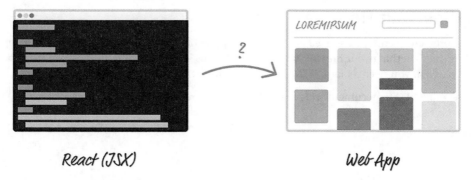

Figure 2.3   JSX needs to turn into something our browser understands.

If we don't do this, our React app simply won't work. That's not cool. Fortunately, we have two solutions to this:

1. **Set up a development environment around Node and a handful of build-tools.** In this environment, every time you perform a build, all of your JSX is automatically converted into JS and placed on disk for you to reference like any plain JavaScript file.

2. **Let your browser automatically convert JSX to JavaScript at runtime.** You specify your JSX directly, just as you would any old piece of JavaScript, and your browser takes care of the rest.

Both of these solutions have a place in our world, but let's talk about the impact of each.

The first solution, while a bit complicated and time-consuming at first, is *the way* modern web development is done these days. Besides compiling (transpiling, to be more accurate) your JSX to JS, this approach enables you to take advantage of modules, better build tools, and a bunch of other features that make building complex web apps somewhat manageable.

The second solution provides a quick and direct path in which you initially spend more time writing code and less time fiddling with your development environment. To use this solution, all you do is reference a script file. This script file takes care of turning the JSX into JS on page load, and your React app comes to life without you having to do anything special to your development environment.

For our introductory look at React, we are going to use the second solution. You might be wondering why we don't always use the second solution. The reason is that your browser takes a performance hit each time it translates JSX into JS. That is totally acceptable when learning how to use React, but it is totally *not* acceptable when deploying your app for real-life use. Because of that lack of acceptability, we will revisit all of this later, to look at the first solution and how to set up your development environment after you've gotten your feet comfortably wet in React.

Getting Your React On

In the previous section, we looked at the two ways you have for ensuring that your React app ends up as something your browser understands. In this section, we put all those words into practice. First, you need a blank HTML page as your starting point.

Create a new HTML document with the following contents:

```
<!DOCTYPE html>
<html>

<head>
  <meta charset="utf-8">
  <title>React! React! React!</title>
</head>

<body>
  <script>

  </script>
</body>

</html>
```

This page has nothing interesting or exciting going for it, but let's fix that by adding a reference to the React library. Just below the title, add these two lines:

```
<script src="https://unpkg.com/react@16/umd/react.development.js"></script>
<script src="https://unpkg.com/react-dom@16/umd/react-dom.development.js"></script>
```

These two lines bring in both the core React library and the various things React needs to work with the DOM. Without them, you aren't building a React app at all.

Now, you aren't done yet. You need to reference one more library. Just below these two script tags, add the following line:

```
<script src="https://unpkg.com/babel-standalone@6.15.0/babel.min.js"></script>
```

Here you're adding a reference to the Babel JavaScript compiler (http://babeljs.io/). Babel does many cool things, but the one we care about is its capability to turn JSX into JavaScript.

At this point, your HTML page should look as follows:

```
<!DOCTYPE html>
<html>

<head>
  <meta charset="utf-8">
  <title>React! React! React!</title>
  <script src="https://unpkg.com/react@16/umd/react.development.js"></script>
  <script src="https://unpkg.com/react-dom@16/umd/react-dom.development.js"></script>
  <script src="https://unpkg.com/babel-standalone@6.15.0/babel.min.js"></script>
</head>

<body>
  <script>

  </script>
</body>

</html>
```

If you preview your page right now, you'll notice that this page is still blank, with nothing visible going on. That's okay. We're going to fix that next.

Displaying Your Name

Now you're going to use React to display your name onscreen. You do that by using a method called render. Inside your empty script tag in the body, add the following:

```
ReactDOM.render(
  <h1>Sherlock Holmes</h1>,
  document.body
);
```

Don't worry if none of this makes sense at this point. Our goal is to get something to display onscreen first, and we'll make sense of what we did afterward. Now, before previewing this in the page to see what happens, you need to designate this script block as something that Babel can work its magic on. You do that is by setting the type attribute on the script tag to a value of text/babel:

```
<script type="text/babel">
  ReactDOM.render(
    <h1>Sherlock Holmes</h1>,
    document.body
  );
</script>
```

After you've made that change, preview what you have in your browser. You'll see the words Sherlock Holmes printed in giant letters, as in Figure 2.4.

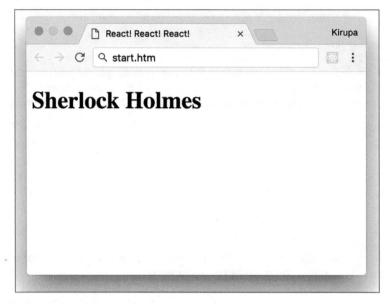

Figure 2.4   Your browser should display Sherlock Holmes.

Congratulations! You've just built an app using React.

As apps go, this isn't all that exciting. Chances are, your name isn't even Sherlock Holmes. This app doesn't have much going for it, but it does introduce you to one of the most frequently used methods you'll use in the React universe: the `ReactDOM.render` method.

The `render` method takes two arguments:

1. The HTML-like elements (a.k.a. JSX) you want to output

2. The location in the DOM where React will render the JSX into

Here's what our `render` method looks like:

```
ReactDOM.render(
  <h1>Sherlock Holmes</h1>,
  document.body
);
```

Our first argument is the text `Sherlock Holmes` wrapped inside some `h1` tags. This HTML-like syntax inside your JavaScript is what JSX is all about. We'll spend a lot more time drilling into JSX a bit later, but I should mention this up front: *It is every bit as crazy as it looks.* Whenever I see brackets and slashes in JavaScript, a part of me dies on the inside because of all the string escaping and quotation mark gibberish I will need to do. With JSX, you do none of that. You just place your HTML-like content as is, just like you've done here. Magically (like the super-awesome kind involving dragons and laser beams), it all works.

The second argument is `document.body`. There's nothing crazy or bizarre about this argument. It simply specifies where the converted markup from the JSX will end up living in our DOM. In our example, when the `render` method runs, the `h1` tag (and everything inside it) is placed in our document's `body` element.

Now, the goal of this exercise wasn't to display *a* name on the screen. It was to display *your* name. Go ahead and modify your code to do that. In my case, the `render` method will look as follows:

```
ReactDOM.render(
  <h1>Batman</h1>,
  document.body
);
```

Well, it would look like that if my name were Batman! Anyway, if you preview your page now, you'll see your name displayed instead of Sherlock Holmes.

It's All Still Familiar

The JavaScript looks new and shiny thanks to JSX, but the end result your browser sees is nice and clean HTML, CSS, and JavaScript. To see this for yourself, let's make a few alterations to how our app behaves and looks.

Changing the Destination

First we'll change where the JSX gets output. Using JavaScript to place things directly in your `body` element is never a good idea. A lot can go wrong, especially if you're going to be mixing React with other JS libraries and frameworks. The recommended path is to create a separate element that you will treat as a new root element. This element will serve as the destination your `render` method will use. To make this happen, go back to the HTML and add a `div` element with an `id` value of `container`:

```
<body>
  <div id="container"></div>
  <script type="text/babel">
    ReactDOM.render(
      <h1>Batman</h1>,
      document.body
    );
  </script>
</body>
```

With the **container** div element safely defined, let's modify the render method to use it instead of document.body. Here's one way of doing this:

```
ReactDOM.render(
  <h1>Batman</h1>,
  document.querySelector("#container")
);
```

Another option is to do some things outside the render method itself:

```
var destination = document.querySelector("#container");

ReactDOM.render(
  <h1>Batman</h1>,
  destination
);
```

Notice that the destination variable stores the reference to your **container** DOM element. Inside the render method, you simply reference the same destination variable instead of writing the full element-finding syntax as part of the argument itself. The reason for this is simple: I want to show you that you're still writing JavaScript and that render is just another boring old method that happens to take two arguments.

Styling It Up!

Time for the last change before we call it a day. Right now, our names show up in whatever default h1 styling the browser provides. That's just terrible, so let's fix that by adding some CSS. Inside your head tag, let's add a style block with the following CSS:

```
<style>
  #container {
    padding: 50px;
    background-color: #EEE;
  }
  #container h1 {
    font-size: 144px;
    font-family: sans-serif;
    color: #0080A8;
  }
</style>
```

After you've added everything, preview your page. Notice that the text appears to have a little more purpose than it did earlier, when it relied entirely on the browser's default styling (see Figure 2.5).

Figure 2.5   The result of adding the CSS.

This works because, after running all the React code, the DOM's `body` contains our `container` element with an `h1` tag inside it. It doesn't matter that the `h1` tag was defined entirely inside JavaScript in this JSX syntax or that your CSS was defined well outside the `render` method. The end result of your React app is still going to be made up of some 100% organic (and cage-free!) HTML, CSS, and JavaScript. If we had to see what this transpiled JavaScript looks like, it would look a bit like the following:

```
<!DOCTYPE html>
<html>

<head>
  <meta charset="utf-8">
  <title>React! React! React!</title>
  <script src="https://unpkg.com/react@16/umd/react.development.js">
</script>
  <script src="https://unpkg.com/react-dom@16/umd/react-dom.development.js">
</script>
  <script src="https://unpkg.com/babel-standalone@6.15.0/babel.min.js"></script>

  <style>
    #container {
      padding: 50px;
      background-color: #EEE;
    }
    #container h1 {
      font-size: 144px;
      font-family: sans-serif;
      color: #0080A8;
    }
```

```
    </style>
</head>

<body>
  <div id="container"></div>
  <script type="text/babel">
    var destination = document.querySelector("#container");

    ReactDOM.render(React.createElement(
      "h1",
      null,
      "Batman"
    ), destination);
  </script>
</body>

</html>
```

Notice that there's nary a trace of React-like code in sight. (Also, we should use the word *nary* more often in everyday conversation!)

Conclusion

If this is your first time building a React app, we covered a lot of ground here. One of the biggest takeaways is that React is different than other libraries because it uses a whole new language called JSX to define what the visuals will look like. You got a very small glimpse of that here when we defined the `h1` tag inside the `render` method.

JSX's impact goes beyond how you define your UI elements. It also alters how you build your app as a whole. Because your browser can't understand JSX in its native representation, you need to use an intermediate step to convert that JSX into JavaScript. One approach is to build your app to generate the transpiled JavaScript output to correspond to the JSX source. Another approach (the one we used here) is to use the Babel library to translate the JSX into JavaScript on the browser itself. While the performance hit of doing this is not recommended for live/production apps, when you're familiarizing yourself with React, you can't beat the convenience.

In future chapters, we spend some time diving deeper into JSX and going beyond the `render` method as we look at all the important things that make React tick.

> **Note: If you run into any issues, ask!**
>
> If you have any questions or your code isn't running like you expect, don't hesitate to ask! Post on the forums at https://forum.kirupa.com and get help from some of the friendliest and most knowledgeable people the Internet has ever brought together!

3

Components in React

Components are one of the pieces that make React, well, React! They're one of the primary ways you have for defining the visuals and interactions that make up what people see when they use your app. Let's say Figure 3.1 shows what your finished app looks like.

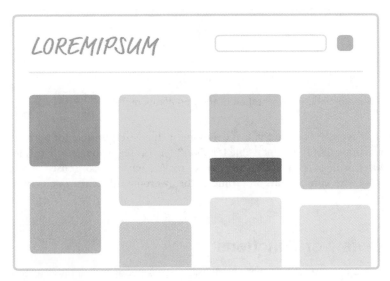

Figure 3.1   Your hypothetical finished app.

This is the finished sausage. During development, viewed through the lens of a React project, things might look a little less appealing. Almost every part of this app's visuals would be wrapped inside a self-contained module known as a **component**. To highlight what "almost every" means here, take a look at the diagram in Figure 3.2.

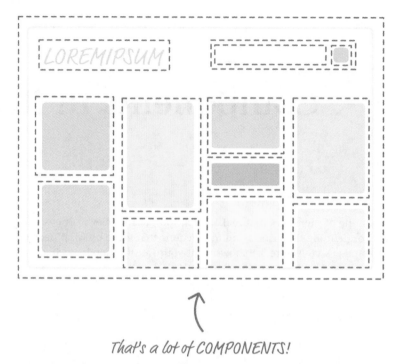

That's a lot of COMPONENTS!

Figure 3.2   Diagrammatic representation of the app components.

Each dotted line represents an individual component that is responsible for both what you see and any interactions that it is responsible for. Don't let this scare you. While this looks really complicated, you will soon see that it will start to make a whole lot of sense once you've had a chance to play with components and some of the awesome things they do—or, at least, try really hard to do.

Quick Review of Functions

In JavaScript, you have **functions** that enable you to make your code a bit cleaner and more reusable. Now, there's reason we're taking some time to look at functions, and it isn't to annoy you! Conceptually, functions share a lot of surface area with React components, and the easiest way to understand what components do is to take a quick look at functions first.

In a terrible world where functions don't exist, you might have some code that looks as follows:

```
var speed = 10;
var time = 5;
alert(speed * time);
```

```
var speed1 = 85;
var time1 = 1.5;
alert(speed1 * time1);

var speed2 = 12;
var time2 = 9;
alert(speed2 * time2);

var speed3 = 42;
var time3 = 21;
alert(speed3 * time3);
```

In a really chill world that involves functions, you can condense all that duplicated text into something simple, like the following:

```
function getDistance(speed, time) {
  var result = speed * time;
  alert(result);
}
```

Our getDistance function removes all the duplicated code you saw earlier, and it takes speed and time as arguments to allow you to customize the calculation that gets returned.

To call this function, all you have to do is this:

```
getDistance(10, 5);
getDistance(85, 1.5);
getDistance(12, 9);
getDistance(42, 21);
```

Doesn't this look nicer? Functions provide another great value, too. Your functions (such as the alert inside getDistance) can call other functions as part of their running. Take a look at using a formatDistance function to change what getDistance returns:

```
function formatDistance(distance) {
  return distance + " km";
}

function getDistance(speed, time) {
  var result = speed * time;
  alert(formatDistance(result));
}
```

This capability to have functions call other functions enables us to cleanly separate what functions do. You don't need to have one monolithic function that does everything under the sun; you can distribute functionality across many functions that are specialized for a particular type of task.

Best of all, after you make changes to how your functions work, you don't have to do anything extra to see the results of those changes. If the function signature didn't change, any existing calls to that function will just magically work and automatically pick up any new changes you made to the function itself.

In a nutshell, functions are awesome. I know that. You know that. That's why all of the code we write has them all over the place.

Changing How We Deal with UI

I don't think anybody will disagree with the good functions bring to the table. They really make it possible to structure the code for your apps in a sane way. That same level of care we use in writing our code isn't always possible when it comes to writing our UIs. For various technical and nontechnical reasons, we've always tolerated a certain level of sloppiness with how we typically work with our UI elements.

That's a pretty controversial statement, so let me highlight what I mean by looking at some examples. Let's go back and look at the render method we used in the previous chapter:

```
var destination = document.querySelector("#container");

ReactDOM.render(
  <h1>Batman</h1>,
  destination
);
```

Onscreen, you see the word **Batman** printed in giant letters, thanks to the h1 element. Let's change things up a bit. Say that we want to print the names of several other superheroes. To do this, we modify our render method to look as follows:

```
var destination = document.querySelector("#container");

ReactDOM.render(
  <div>
    <h1>Batman</h1>
    <h1>Iron Man</h1>
    <h1>Nicolas Cage</h1>
    <h1>Mega Man</h1>
  </div>,
  destination
);
```

Notice what you see here. We emit a div that contains the four h1 elements with our superhero names.

Okay, so now we have four h1 elements that each contains the name of a superhero. What if we want to change our h1 element to something like an h3 instead? We can manually update all of these elements as follows:

```
var destination = document.querySelector("#container");

ReactDOM.render(
  <div>
    <h3>Batman</h3>
    <h3>Iron Man</h3>
```

```
    <h3>Nicolas Cage</h3>
    <h3>Mega Man</h3>
  </div>,
  destination
);
```

If you preview what we have, you'll see something that looks a bit unstyled and plain (see Figure 3.3).

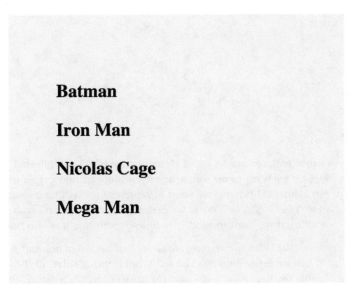

Batman

Iron Man

Nicolas Cage

Mega Man

Figure 3.3   Plain vanilla superhero names.

We don't want to go crazy with the styling here. All we want to do is italicize all these names by using the i tag, so let's manually update what we render by making this change:

```
var destination = document.querySelector("#container");

ReactDOM.render(
  <div>
    <h3><i>Batman</i></h3>
    <h3><i>Iron Man</i></h3>
    <h3><i>Nicolas Cage</i></h3>
    <h3><i>Mega Man</i></h3>
  </div>,
  destination
);
```

We went through each h3 element and wrapped the content inside some i tags. Can you start to see the problem here? What we are doing with our UI is no different than having code that looks as follows:

```
var speed = 10;
var time = 5;
alert(speed * time);

var speed1 = 85;
var time1 = 1.5;
alert(speed1 * time1);

var speed2 = 12;
var time2 = 9;
alert(speed2 * time2);

var speed3 = 42;
var time3 = 21;
alert(speed3 * time3);
```

Every change we want to make to our h1 or h3 elements needs to be duplicated for every instance of them. What if we want to do something even more complex than just modifying the appearance of our elements? What if we want to represent something more complex than the simple examples we're using so far? What we're doing right now won't scale; manually updating every copy of what we want to modify is time-consuming. It is also boring.

Now, here's a crazy thought: *What if everything awesome that we looked at about functions could somehow be applied to how we define our app's visuals?* Wouldn't that solve all the inefficiencies we've highlighted in this section? As it turns out, the answer to that "what if" forms the core of what React is all about. It's time for you to say hello to the **component**.

Meet the React Component

The solution to all of our problems (even the existential ones we grapple with) can be found in React components. *React components are reusable chunks of JavaScript that output (via JSX) HTML elements.* That sounds really pedestrian for something capable of solving great things, but as you start to build components and gradually turn up the complexity, you'll see that components are really powerful and every bit as awesome as I've portrayed them.

Let's start by building a couple of components together. To follow along, start with a blank React document:

```
<!DOCTYPE html>
<html>

<head>
  <meta charset="utf-8">
  <title>React Components</title>
```

```
<script src="https://unpkg.com/react@16/umd/react.development.js"></script>
<script src="https://unpkg.com/react-dom@16/umd/react-dom.development.js"></script>
<script src="https://unpkg.com/babel-standalone@6.15.0/babel.min.js"></script>
</head>

<body>
  <div id="container"></div>
  <script type="text/babel">

  </script>
</body>

</html>
```

Nothing exciting is going on in this page. As in the last chapter, this page is pretty barebones, with just a reference to the React and Babel libraries and a div element that proudly sports an id value of container.

Creating a Hello, World! Component

Let's start really simple. We want to use a component to help us print the famous "Hello, world!" text to the screen. As we already know, using just the render method of ReactDOM would give us code that looks as follows:

```
ReactDOM.render(
  <div>
    <p>Hello, world!</p>
  </div>,
  document.querySelector("#container")
);
```

Let's re-create all of this by using a component. React gives us several ways of creating components, but we are going to create them by using the class syntax. Go ahead and add the following highlighted code just above the existing render method:

```
class HelloWorld extends React.Component {

}

ReactDOM.render(
  <div>
    <p>Hello, world!</p>
  </div>,
  document.querySelector("#container")
);
```

If the class syntax is foreign to you, first check out my online tutorial Using Classes in JavaScript (https://www.kirupa.com/javascript/classy_way_to_create_objects.htm).

Getting back to our code, we have created a new component called `HelloWorld`. This is a component because it extends `React.Component`. If it didn't do that, it would just be an empty class that doesn't do much. Inside our class, you can put all sorts of methods to further define what HelloWorld does. Some methods that you define are special, and React uses them to help your components work their magic. One such mandatory property is `render`.

Go ahead and modify our `HelloWorld` component by adding the `render` method, as shown:

```
class HelloWorld extends React.Component {
  render() {

  }
}
```

Just like the `render` method you saw a few moments earlier as part of `ReactDOM.render`, the render function inside a component is also responsible for dealing with JSX. Let's modify our render function to return **Hello, componentized world!**. Add the following highlighted line:

```
class HelloWorld extends React.Component {
  render() {
    return <p>Hello, componentized world!</p>
  }
}
```

You've told the `render` function to return the JSX that represents the **Hello, componentized world!** text. All that remains is to actually use this component. You use a component after you've defined it by **calling** it. Here we call it from our old friend, the `ReactDOM.render` method.

The way you call a component from it is a bit unique. Go ahead and replace the first argument to `ReactDOM.render` with the following:

```
ReactDOM.render(
  <HelloWorld/>,
  document.querySelector("#container")
);
```

That isn't a typo! The JSX we use for calling our HelloWorld component is the very HTML-like `<HelloWorld/>`. If you preview your page in your browser, you'll see the text **Hello, componentized world!** showing up on your screen. If you were holding your breath in suspense, you can relax.

If you have difficulty relaxing after seeing the syntax we used for calling `HelloWorld`, stare at the circle in Figure 3.4 a few moments.

Just relax and focus on this circle!

Figure 3.4   Just some lighthearted distraction!

Okay, back to reality. What we've done so far might seem crazy, but simply think of your `<HelloWorld/>` component as a cool and new HTML tag whose functionality you fully have control over. This means you can do all sorts of HTML-y things to it.

For example, go ahead and modify our `ReactDOM.render` method to look as follows:

```
ReactDOM.render(
  <div>
    <HelloWorld/>
  </div>,
  document.querySelector("#container")
);
```

We wrapped our call to the `HelloWorld` component inside a `div` element, and if you preview this in your browser, everything still works. Let's go one step further! Instead of having just a single call to `HelloWorld`, let's make a bunch of calls. Modify our `ReactDOM.render` method to now look as follows:

```
ReactDOM.render(
  <div>
    <HelloWorld/>
    <HelloWorld/>
    <HelloWorld/>
    <HelloWorld/>
    <HelloWorld/>
    <HelloWorld/>
  </div>,
  document.querySelector("#container")
);
```

Now you'll see is a bunch of **Hello, componentized world!** text instances appear. Let's do one more thing before we move on to something shinier. Go back to our `HelloWorld` component declaration and change the text you return to the more traditional **Hello, world!** value:

```
class HelloWorld extends React.Component {
  render() {
    return <p>Hello, world!</p>
  }
}
```

Make this one change and then preview your example. This time around, all the various `HelloWorld` calls we specified earlier return **Hello, world!** to the screen. No need to manually modify every `HelloWorld` call—that's a good thing!

Specifying Properties

Right now, our component does just one thing. It prints **Hello, world!** to the screen—and only that! That's the equivalent of having a JavaScript function that looks like this:

```
function getDistance() {
  alert("42km");
}
```

Except for one very specific case, that JavaScript function doesn't seem very useful, does it? To increase the usefulness of this function, we need to modify it to take arguments:

```
function getDistance(speed, time) {
  var result = speed * time;
  alert(result);
}
```

Now this function can be used more generally for a variety of situations, not just one whose output will be **42km**.

Something similar applies to your components as well. Just as with functions, you can pass in arguments that alter what your component does. There's a slight terminology update you need to be on top of. What we call **arguments** in the function world are known as **properties** in the component world. Let's see these properties in action!

You're now going to modify the `HelloWorld` component to allow you to specify who or what you greet besides the generic **World**. For example, imagine being able to specify **Bono** as part of the `HelloWorld` call and seeing **Hello, Bono!** appear onscreen.

To add properties to a component, you need to follow two parts of instructions.

First Part: Updating the Component Definition

Right now, our `HelloWorld` component is hard-coded to always send out **Hello, world!** as part of its return value. We first need to change that behavior by having the *return* statement print out the value passed in by a property. We need a name to give our property; for this example, we call our property `greetTarget`.

To specify the value of `greetTarget` as part of our component, we need to make this modification:

```
class HelloWorld extends React.Component {
  render() {
    return <p>Hello, {this.props.greetTarget}!</p>
  }
}
```

You access a property by referencing it via the `this.props` property that every component has access to. Notice how you specify this property: You place it inside curly brackets, { and }. *In JSX, if you want something to get evaluated as an expression, you need to wrap that something inside curly brackets.* If you don't do that, you'll see the raw text `this.props.greetTarget` printed out.

Second Part: Modifying the Component Call

After you've updated the component definition, all that remains is to pass in the property value as part of the component call. This is done by adding an attribute with the same name as the property, followed by the value you want to pass in. In our example, that involves modifying the `HelloWorld` call with the `greetTarget` attribute and the value you want to give it.

Go ahead and modify the `HelloWorld` calls as follows:

```
ReactDOM.render(
  <div>
    <HelloWorld greetTarget="Batman"/>
    <HelloWorld greetTarget="Iron Man"/>
    <HelloWorld greetTarget="Nicolas Cage"/>
    <HelloWorld greetTarget="Mega Man"/>
    <HelloWorld greetTarget="Bono"/>
    <HelloWorld greetTarget="Catwoman"/>
  </div>,
  document.querySelector("#container")
);
```

Each `HelloWorld` call now has the `greetTarget` attribute, along with the name of a super-hero (or equivalent mythical being) that we want to greet. If you preview this example in the browser, you'll see the greetings happily printed out onscreen.

One last point is important to call out before we move on. You are not limited to having just a single property on a component. You can have as many properties as you want, and your props property will easily accommodate any property requests you have without making any fuss.

Dealing with Children

A few sections ago, I mentioned that components (in JSX) are very similar to regular HTML elements. You saw that when you wrapped a component inside a `div` element or specified an attribute and value as part of specifying properties. *Just as you can have many HTML elements, your components can have children.*

This means you can do something like this:

```
<CleverComponent foo="bar">
  <p>Something!</p>
</CleverComponent>
```

Here you have a component very cleverly called `CleverComponent`, and it has a `p` element as a child. From within `CleverComponent`, you have the capability to access the `p` child element (and any children it has) via the `children` property accessed by `this.props.children`.

To make sense of all this, let's look at another really simple example. This time around, we have a component called `Buttonify` that wraps its children inside a button. The component looks like this:

```
class Buttonify extends React.Component {
  render() {
    return(
      <div>
        <button type={this.props.behavior}>{this.props.children}</button>
      </div>
    );
  }
}
```

You can use this component by calling it via the `ReactDOM.render` method, as shown here:

```
ReactDOM.render(
  <div>
    <Buttonify behavior="submit">SEND DATA</Buttonify>
  </div>,
  document.querySelector("#container")
);
```

When this code runs, given what the JSX in the `Buttonify` component's render method looked like, you see the words **SEND DATA** wrapped inside a button element. With the appropriate styling, the result could look comically large, as in Figure 3.5.

Figure 3.5   A large Send Data button.

Getting back to the JSX, notice that we specify a custom property called behavior. This property allows us to specify the button element's type attribute, and you can see us accessing it via `this.props.behavior` in the component definition's `render` method.

There's more to accessing a component's children than what you've seen here. For example, if your child element is just some text, the `this.props.children` property returns a string. If your child element is just a single element (as in our example), the `this.props.children` property returns a single component that is *not* wrapped inside an array. We still need to call out a few more things, but instead of enumerating all the cases and boring you, we'll bring up those points later as we look at more elaborate examples.

Conclusion

If you want to build an app using React, you can't wander too far without having to use a component. Trying to build a React app without using a component is kind of like building a JavaScript-based app without using functions. I'm not saying that it can't be done; it's just one of those things you don't do—kind of like the *Bad Idea* part of the popular Animaniacs Good Idea/Bad Idea sketches (https://www.youtube.com/watch?v=2dJOIf4mdus).

If this witty video doesn't convince you that you should learn to embrace components, I don't know what will—except for maybe a future chapter on creating complex components!

> **Note: If you run into any issues, ask!**
>
> If you have any questions or your code isn't running like you expect, don't hesitate to ask! Post on the forums at https://forum.kirupa.com and get help from some of the friendliest and most knowledgeable people the Internet has ever brought together!

4

Styling in React

For generations, mankind (and probably really smart dolphins) has styled HTML content using CSS. Things were good. CSS had good separation between content and presentation. The selector syntax offered a lot of flexibility in choosing which elements to style and which ones to skip. We couldn't even find many reasons to hate the *whole cascading thing* CSS is all about.

Well, don't tell React that. React doesn't actively hate CSS, but it has a different view when it comes to styling content. As you've seen, one of React's core ideas is to make an app's visual pieces self-contained and reusable. That's why the HTML elements and the JavaScript that impacts them are in the same bucket, called a **component**. You got a taste of that in the previous chapter.

What about how the HTML elements look (a.k.a. their styling)? Where should they go? You can probably guess where we're going with this. You can't have a self-contained piece of UI when the styling for it is defined somewhere else. That's why React encourages you to specify how your elements look right alongside the HTML and the JavaScript. In this tutorial, you'll learn all about this mysterious (and possibly scandalous) approach for styling your content. Of course, we also look at how to use CSS. There's room for both approaches, even if React might sort of, kind of not think so.

Displaying Some Vowels

To learn how to style React content, let's work together on a (totally sweet and exciting) example that simply displays vowels on a page. First, you'll need a blank HTML page that will host your React content. Create a new HTML document and add the following content into it:

```
<!DOCTYPE html>
<html>

<head>
  <meta charset="utf-8">
  <title>Styling in React</title>
  <script src="https://unpkg.com/react@16/umd/react.development.js"></script>
```

```
    <script src="https://unpkg.com/react-dom@16/umd/react-dom.development.js"></script>
    <script src="https://unpkg.com/babel-standalone@6.15.0/babel.min.js"></script>

    <style>
      #container {
        padding: 50px;
        background-color: #FFF;
      }
    </style>
  </head>

<body>
  <div id="container"></div>

</body>

</html>
```

To display the vowels, you need to add some React-specific code. Just below the **container** div element, add the following:

```
<script type="text/babel">
  var destination = document.querySelector("#container");

  class Letter extends React.Component {
    render() {
      return(
        <div>
          {this.props.children}
        </div>
      );
    }
  }

  ReactDOM.render(
    <div>
      <Letter>A</Letter>
      <Letter>E</Letter>
      <Letter>I</Letter>
      <Letter>O</Letter>
      <Letter>U</Letter>
    </div>,
    destination
  );
</script>
```

From what you learned about components earlier, nothing here should be a mystery. You're creating a component called `Letter` that is responsible for wrapping your vowels inside a `div` element.

If you preview your page, you'll see something boring that looks like Figure 4.1.

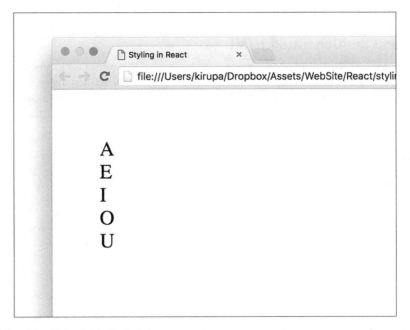

Figure 4.1   A boring output of what you see.

Don't worry, you'll make it look a little less boring in a few moments. After you've had a run at these letters, you'll see something that looks more like Figure 4.2.

Figure 4.2   What our result looks like with some styling applied!

The vowels will be wrapped in a yellow background, aligned horizontally, with a fancy monospace font. Let's look at how to do all of this both in CSS and using React's newfangled approach.

Styling React Content Using CSS

Using CSS to style React content is actually as straightforward as you can imagine it to be. Because React ends up spitting out regular HTML tags, all of the various CSS tricks you've learned over the years for styling HTML still apply. You just need to keep a few minor points in mind.

Understand the Generated HTML

Before you can use CSS, you need to get a feel for how the HTML that React spits out is going to look. You can easily figure that out by looking at the JSX defined inside the render methods. The parent render method is our ReactDOM-based one, and it looks as follows:

```
<div>
  <Letter>A</Letter>
  <Letter>E</Letter>
  <Letter>I</Letter>
  <Letter>O</Letter>
  <Letter>U</Letter>
</div>
```

We have our various Letter components wrapped inside a div. Nothing too exciting here. The render method inside our Letter component isn't that much different, either:

```
<div>
  {this.props.children}
</div>
```

As you can see, each individual vowel is wrapped inside its own set of div tags. If you play this all out (such as previewing our example in a browser), the final DOM structure for our vowels would look like Figure 4.3.

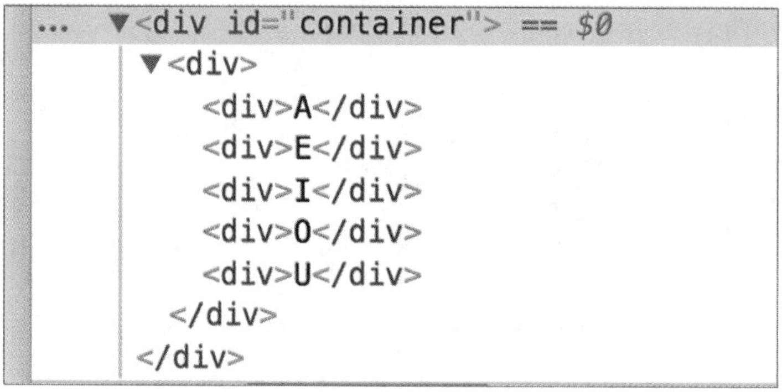

```
...    ▼<div id="container"> == $0
       ▼<div>
           <div>A</div>
           <div>E</div>
           <div>I</div>
           <div>O</div>
           <div>U</div>
         </div>
       </div>
```

Figure 4.3 The preview from inside the browser.

We have simply an HTML-ized expansion of the various JSX fragments you saw in the `render` method a few moments ago, with our **vowels nested** inside a bunch of `div` elements.

Just Style It Already!

When you understand the HTML arrangement of the things you want to style, the hard part is done. Now comes the fun and familiar part of defining style selectors and specifying the properties you want to set. To affect the inner `div` elements, add the following inside the style tag:

```
div div div {
  padding: 10px;
  margin: 10px;
  background-color: #FFDE00;
  color: #333;
  display: inline-block;
  font-family: monospace;
  font-size: 32px;
  text-align: center;
}
```

The `div div div` selector ensures that we style the right things. The end result will be our vowels styled to look exactly like we set out to. With that said, a style selector of `div div div` looks a bit odd, doesn't it? It's too generic. In apps with more than three `div` elements (which is common), you can end up styling the wrong things. At times like these, you will want to change the HTML that React generates to make the content more easily styleable.

We address this by giving our inner `div` elements a class value of `letter`. Here is where JSX differs from HTML. Make the following highlighted change:

```
class Letter extends React.Component {
  render() {
    return (
      <div className="letter">
        {this.props.children}
      </div>
    );
  }
}
```

Notice that we designate the class value by using the `className` attribute instead of the `class` attribute. This is because the word *class* is a special keyword in JavaScript. If that doesn't make any sense, don't worry about it for now; we'll cover it later.

After you've given your `div` a `className` attribute value of `letter`, there's just one more thing to do. Modify the CSS selector to target the `div` elements more cleanly:

```
.letter {
  padding: 10px;
  margin: 10px;
```

```
  background-color: #FFDE00;
  color: #333;
  display: inline-block;
  font-family: monospace;
  font-size: 32px;
  text-align: center;
}
```

As you can see, using CSS is a perfectly viable way to style the content in your React-based apps. In the next section, we look at how to style content using the approach React prefers.

Styling Content the React Way

React favors an inline approach for styling content that doesn't use CSS. That might seem a bit strange at first, but it's designed to make your visuals more reusable. The goal is to make your components little black boxes where everything related to how your UI looks and works is stashed. Let's see this in action.

Continuing our example from earlier, remove the .letter style rule. Your vowels will return to their unstyled state when you preview your app in the browser. For completeness, you should also remove the className declaration from the Letter component's render function. There's no point having your markup contain pieces you won't be using.

Now let's revert the Letter component to its original state:

```
class Letter extends React.Component {
  render() {
    return (
      <div>
        {this.props.children}
      </div>
    );
  }
}
```

You specify styles inside your component by defining an object whose content is the CSS properties and their values. When you have that object, you assign that object to the JSX elements you want to style by using the style attribute. This will make more sense when you perform these two steps yourself, so let's apply all of this to style the output of the Letter component.

Creating a Style Object

Let's get right to it by defining our object that contains the styles we want to apply:

```
class Letter extends React.Component {
  render() {
    var letterStyle = {
      padding: 10,
      margin: 10,
```

```
      backgroundColor: "#FFDE00",
      color: "#333",
      display: "inline-block",
      fontFamily: "monospace",
      fontSize: 32,
      textAlign: "center"
    };

    return (
      <div>
        {this.props.children}
      </div>
    );
  }
}
```

We have an object called letterStyle, and the properties inside it are just CSS property names and their value. If you've never defined CSS properties in JavaScript (by setting object.style), the formula for converting them into something JavaScript-friendly is pretty simple:

1. Single-word CSS properties (such as padding, margin, and color) remain unchanged.

2. Multiword CSS properties with a dash in them (such as background-color, font-family, and border-radius) are turned into one camel-case word, with the dash removed and the first letter of the second word capitalized. For example, using our example properties, background-color becomes backgroundColor, font-family becomes fontFamily, and border-radius becomes borderRadius.

Our letterStyle object and its properties are pretty much a direct JavaScript translation of the .letter style rule we looked at a few moments ago. All that remains now is to assign this object to the element we want to style.

Actually Styling Our Content

Now that we have our object containing the styles we want to apply, the rest is easy. Find the element you want to apply the style on and set the style attribute to refer to that object. In our case, that is the div element returned by our Letter component's render function.

Take a look at the highlighted line to see how this is done for our example:

```
class Letter extends React.Component {
  render() {
    var letterStyle = {
      padding: 10,
      margin: 10,
      backgroundColor: "#FFDE00",
```

```
      color: "#333",
      display: "inline-block",
      fontFamily: "monospace",
      fontSize: 32,
      textAlign: "center"
    };

    return (
      <div>
        {this.props.children}
      </div>
    );
  }
}
```

Our object is called `letterStyle`, so that's what we specify inside the curly brackets to let React know to evaluate the expression. That's all there is to it. Go ahead and run the example in the browser to ensure that everything works properly and that all the vowels are properly styled.

For extra validation, if you inspect the styling applied to one of the vowels using your browser developer tool of choice, you'll see that the styles are, in fact, applied inline (see Figure 4.4).

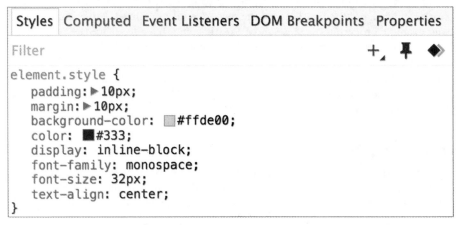

Figure 4.4   The styles are applied inline.

While this is no surprise, it might be difficult to adjust to if you're used to styles being inside style rules. As they say, the times are a-changin'.

Making the Background Color Customizable

The last thing to do before we wrap up is take advantage of how React works with styles. By having our styles defined in the same vicinity as the JSX, we can make the various style values easily customizable by the parent (a.k.a. the consumer of the component). Let's see this in action.

Right now, all of our vowels have a yellow background. Wouldn't it be cool if we could specify the background color as part of each `Letter` declaration? To do this in our `ReactDOM.render` method, first add a `bgcolor` attribute and specify some colors, as shown in the following highlighted lines:

```
ReactDOM.render(
    <div>
        <Letter bgcolor="#58B3FF">A</Letter>
        <Letter bgcolor="#FF605F">E</Letter>
        <Letter bgcolor="#FFD52E">I</Letter>
        <Letter bgcolor="#49DD8E">O</Letter>
        <Letter bgcolor="#AE99FF">U</Letter>
    </div>,
    destination
);
```

Next, we need to use this property. In the `letterStyle` object, set the value of `backgroundColor` to `this.props.bgColor`:

```
var letterStyle = {
  padding: 10,
  margin: 10,
  backgroundColor: this.props.bgcolor,
  color: "#333",
  display: "inline-block",
  fontFamily: "monospace",
  fontSize: 32,
  textAlign: "center"
};
```

This ensures that the `backgroundColor` value is inferred from what you set via the `bgColor` attribute as part of the `Letter` declaration. If you preview this in your browser, you will now see the same vowels sporting some totally sweet background colors (see Figure 4.5).

Figure 4.5   Our vowels with background colors!

What we've just done will be very hard to replicate using plain CSS. As we start to look at components whose contents change based on state or user interaction, you'll see more such examples in which the React way of styling things has a lot of merit.

Conclusion

As you dive in deeper and learn more about React, you'll see several more cases in which React does things quite differently than what you've been told is correct on the web. In this tutorial, you saw React promoting inline styles in JavaScript as a way to style content instead of using CSS style rules. Earlier, we looked at JSX and showed how to declare the entirety of your UI in JavaScript using an XML-like syntax that sort of, kind of looks like HTML.

In all of these cases, if you look deeper beneath the surface, the reasons React diverges from conventional wisdom make a lot of sense. Building apps with their very complex UI requirements necessitate a new way of solving the challenges. HTML, CSS, and JavaScript techniques that probably made a lot of sense when dealing with web pages and documents might not be applicable in a web-app world where components are reused inside other components.

With that said, you need to pick and choose the techniques that make the most sense for your situation. I'm biased toward React's way of solving UI development problems, but I do my best to highlight alternate or conventional methods as well. Tying that back to what you saw here, using CSS style rules with your React content is totally okay, as long as you make the decision knowing both what you gain and what you lose.

> ### Note: If you run into any issues, ask!
>
> If you have any questions or your code isn't running like you expect, don't hesitate to ask! Post on the forums at https://forum.kirupa.com and get help from some of the friendliest and most knowledgeable people the Internet has ever brought together!

5

Creating Complex Components

In Chapter 3, "Components in React," you learned about components and all the awesome things that they do. You learned that components are the primary ways through which React enables our visual elements to behave like little reusable bricks that contain all the HTML, JavaScript, and styling needed to run themselves. Beyond reusability, components bring another major advantage to the table. They make possible **composability**. You can combine components to create more complex components.

In this chapter, we look at what all of this means. More specifically, we look at two points:

- The boring technical stuff you need to know
- The boring stuff you need to know to identify components when you look at a bunch of visual elements

Okay, what you're going to learn isn't actually *that* boring. I'm just setting your expectations really low.

From Visuals to Components

The examples we've looked at so far have been pretty basic. They were great for highlighting technical concepts, but they weren't great for preparing you for the real world.

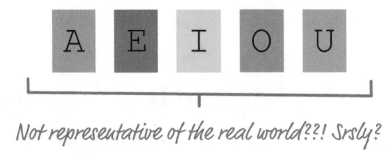

Not representative of the real world??! Srsly?

In the real world, what you'll be asked to implement in React will never be as simple as a list of names or colorful blocks of vowels. Instead, you'll be given a visual of some complex user interface, such as a scribble, diagram, screenshot, video, redline, or comp. Then it'll be up to you to bring all those static pixels to life. You'll get some hands-on practice in this chapter doing just that.

The task here is to build a simple color palette card (see Figure 5.1).

Figure 5.1   A simple color palette card.

Color palette cards are small rectangular cards that help you match a color with a particular type of paint. You can see them in home improvement stores or anywhere paint is sold. Your designer friend probably has a giant closet dedicated to them in his or her place. Anyway, our mission is to re-create one of these cards using React.

We could go about this in several ways, but let's take a systematic approach that simplifies and make sense of even the most complex user interfaces. This approach involves two steps:

1. Identify the major visual elements.

2. Figure out what the components will be.

Both of these steps sound really complex, but as we walk through this, you'll see that you have nothing to worry about.

Identifying the Major Visual Elements

The first step is to identify all the visual elements we're dealing with. No visual element is too minor to omit—at least, not initially. The easiest way to identify the relevant pieces is to start with the obvious visual elements and then dive into the less obvious ones.

The first thing you will see in our example is the card itself (see Figure 5.2).

Figure 5.2 The card.

Within the card are two distinct regions. The top region is a square area that displays a particular color. The bottom region is a white area that displays a hex value.

Let's call out these two visual elements and arrange them into a treelike structure, as shown in Figure 5.3.

Figure 5.3   Treelike structure.

Arranging your visuals into this treelike structure (a.k.a. a **visual hierarchy**) is a good way to get a better feel for how your visual elements are grouped. The goal of this exercise is to identify the important visual elements and break them into a parent/child arrangement until you can divide them no further.

Try to Ignore Implementation Details

It might be hard, but don't think about the implementation details yet. Don't focus on dividing your visual elements based on what combination of HTML and CSS is required. You'll have plenty of time for that later.

Continuing on, we can see that our colorful square isn't something we can divide further. That doesn't mean we're done, though. We can further divide the label from the white region that surrounds it. Right now, our visual hierarchy looks as shown in Figure 5.4, with our label and white region occupying a separate spot in our tree.

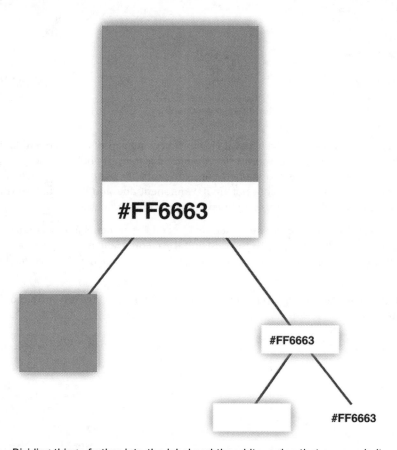

Figure 5.4   Dividing things further into the label and the white region that surrounds it.

At this point, we have nothing else to divide any further. We're finished identifying and dividing up our visual elements, so the next step is to use what we've found to help us identify the components.

Identifying the Components

This is where things get a little interesting. We need to figure out which of the visual elements we've identified will be turned into components and which ones will not. Not every visual element needs to be turned into a component, and we also don't want to create only a few extremely complex components. We need to strike a balance (see Figure 5.5).

Figure 5.5   Not too few and not too many components.

There's an art to figuring out which visual elements become part of a component and which don't. *The general rule is that components should do just one thing.* If you find that your potential component will end up doing too many things, you probably want to break it into multiple components. On the flipside, if your potential component does too little, you probably want to skip making that visual element a component altogether.

Let's try to figure out which elements would make good components in our example. From looking at our visual hierarchy, both the card and the colored square seem like they fit the bill for making a great component. The card acts as the outer container, and the colored square simply displays a color.

That just puts a question mark around our label and the white region it is surrounded by (see Figure 5.6).

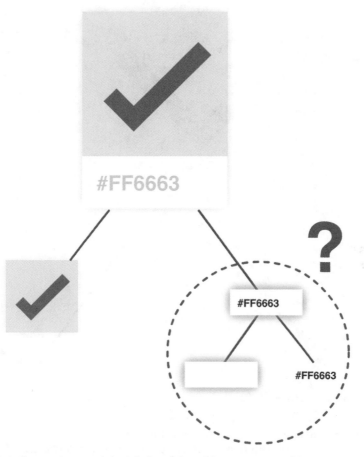

Figure 5.6   Question mark around the label and the white space around it.

The important part here is the label itself. Without it, we can't see the hex value. That leaves just the white region. It serves a negligible purpose; it is simply empty space, and that responsibility can easily be handed off to our label itself. Brace yourself for what I'm about to say next: Sadly, our white rectangular region will not be turned into a component.

At this point, we have identified our three components, and the **component hierarchy** looks like Figure 5.7.

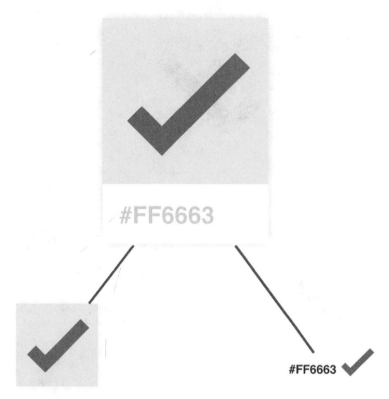

Figure 5.7   The three components.

An important point to note is that the component hierarchy has more to do with helping us define our code than it does with how the finished product will look. You'll notice that it looks a bit different than the visual hierarchy we started with. For visual details, always refer to your source material (a.k.a. your visual comps, redlines, screenshots, and other related items). To figure out which components to create, you should use the component hierarchy.

Okay, now that we've identified our components and the relationships among all of them, it's time to start bringing our color palette card to life.

Creating the Components

This is the easy part...sort of! It's time to start writing some code. First we need a mostly empty HTML page that will serve as our starting point:

```
<!DOCTYPE html>
<html>
```

```
<head>
  <meta charset="utf-8">
  <title>More Components</title>
  <script src="https://unpkg.com/react@16/umd/react.development.js"></script>
  <script src="https://unpkg.com/react-dom@16/umd/react-dom.development.js"></script>
  <script src="https://unpkg.com/babel-standalone@6.15.0/babel.min.js"></script>

  <style>
    #container {
      padding: 50px;
      background-color: #FFF;
    }
  </style>
</head>

<body>
  <div id="container"></div>

  <script type="text/babel">
    ReactDOM.render(
      <div>

      </div>,
      document.querySelector("#container")
    );
  </script>
</body>

</html>
```

Take a moment to see what this page has going on. There isn't much: just the bare minimum needed to have React render an empty div into our **container** element.

After you've done this, it's time to define our three components. The names we'll go with for our components are **Card**, **Label**, and **Square**. Go ahead and add the following lines just above the ReactDOM.render function:

```
class Square extends React.Component {
  render() {
    return(
      <br/>
    );
  }
}
```

```
class Label extends React.Component {
  render() {
    return (
      <br/>
    );
  }
}

class Card extends React.Component {
  render() {
    return (
      <br/>
    );
  }
}
```

Besides declaring our three components, we threw in the render function that each component absolutely needs to function. Each render function returns a simple br element for now; leaving the return value for the render function empty throws an error. Other than that, our components are empty. In the following sections, we'll fix that by filling them in.

The Card Component

Let's start at the top of our component hierarchy and first focus on our Card component. This component will act as the container where our Square and Label components will live.

To implement it, go ahead and make the following highlighted modifications:

```
class Card extends React.Component {
  render() {
    var cardStyle = {
      height: 200,
      width: 150,
      padding: 0,
      backgroundColor: "#FFF",
      boxShadow: "0px 0px 5px #666"
    };

    return (
      <div style={cardStyle}>

      </div>
    );
  }
}
```

This seems like a lot of changes, but most of the lines are going into styling the output of our Card component via the cardStyle object. The rest of the changes are pretty unimpressive. We return a div element, and that element's style attribute is set to our cardStyle object. Now, to see our Card component in action, we need to display it in our DOM as part of the ReactDOM.render function. To make that happen, go ahead and make the following high-lighted change:

```
ReactDOM.render(
  <div>
    <Card/>
  </div>,
  document.querySelector("#container")
);
```

All we're doing is telling the ReactDOM.render function to render the output of our Card component by invoking it. If everything worked out properly, you'll see a result identical to Figure 5.8 if you test your app.

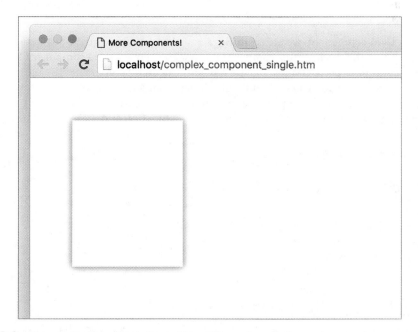

Figure 5.8   The result of your test, the outline of the color palette card.

Yes, it's just the outline of the color palette card, but that's definitely more than what you started with just a few moments ago!

The Square Component

It's time to go one level down in our component hierarchy and look at our Square component. This is a pretty straightforward one, so make the following highlighted changes:

```
class Square extends React.Component {
  render() {
    var squareStyle = {
      height: 150,
      backgroundColor: "#FF6663"
    };

    return (
      <div style={squareStyle}>

      </div>
    );
  }
}
```

As with our Card component, we are returning a `div` element whose `style` attribute is set to a style object that defines how this component looks. To see our Square component in action, we need to get it onto our DOM just like we did with the Card component. The difference this time around is that we won't be calling the Square component via our `ReactDOM.render` function. Instead, we'll call the Square component from inside the Card component. To see what I mean, go back to our Card component's `render` function and make the following change:

```
class Card extends React.Component {
  render() {
    var cardStyle = {
      height: 200,
      width: 150,
      padding: 0,
      backgroundColor: "#FFF",
      boxShadow: "0px 0px 5px #666"
    };

    return (
      <div style={cardStyle}>
        <Square />
      </div>
    );
  }
}
```

At this point, if you preview your app, you'll see a colorful square making an appearance (see Figure 5.9).

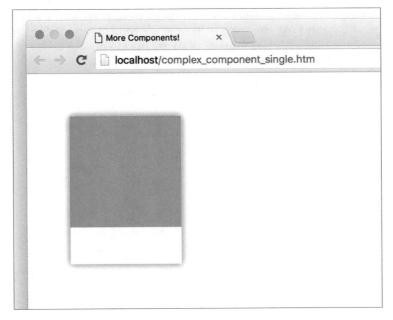

Figure 5.9   The red portion appears.

The cool thing to call out is that we called our Square component from inside the Card compo-nent! This is an example of **component composability**, in which one component relies on the output of another component. The final thing you see is the result of these two components colluding with each other. Isn't collusion just beautiful…at least in this context?

The Label Component

The last component that remains is our Label. Go ahead and make the following highlighted changes:

```
class Label extends React.Component {
  render() {
    var labelStyle = {
      fontFamily: "sans-serif",
      fontWeight: "bold",
      padding: 13,
      margin: 0
    };

    return (
      <p style={labelStyle}>#FF6663</p>
    );
  }
}
```

The pattern of what we're doing should be routine to you by now. We have a style object that we assign to what we return. We return a p element whose content is the string #FF6663. To have what we return ultimately make it to our DOM, we need to call our Label component via our Card component. Go ahead and make the following highlighted change:

```
class Card extends React.Component {
  render() {
    var cardStyle = {
      height: 200,
      width: 150,
      padding: 0,
      backgroundColor: "#FFF",
      boxShadow: "0px 0px 5px #666"
    };

    return (
      <div style={cardStyle}>
        <Square />
        <Label />
      </div>
    );
  }
}
```

Notice that our Label component lives just under the Square component we added to our Card component's return function earlier. If you preview your app in the browser now, you should see something that looks like Figure 5.10.

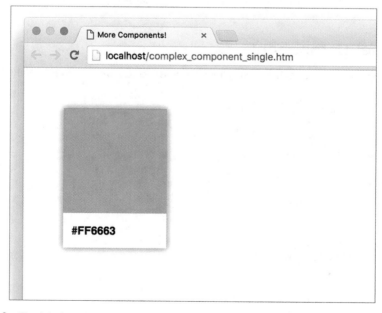

Figure 5.10 The label appears.

Yes, that's right! Our color palette card is done and visible, thanks to the efforts of our Card, Square, and Label components. That doesn't mean we're done yet, though. We have a few more things to cover.

Passing Properties, Again!

In our current example, we hard-coded the color value used by our Square and Label components. That's an odd thing to do. It might or might not have been done deliberately for dramatic effect, but fixing it is straightforward. The solution just involves specifying a property name and accessing it via `this.props`. You've seen all this before; the only difference is the number of times you have to do this.

There's no way to *properly* specify a property on a parent component and have all descendants automatically gain access to that property. There are many *improper* ways to deal with this, such as defining global objects and directly setting the value on a component property. We won't concern ourselves with such improper solutions right now, though. We aren't animals!

The proper way to pass a property value to a child component is to have each intermediate parent component pass on the property as well. To see this in action, take a look at the highlighted changes to our current code. We move away from a hard-coded color and instead define our card's color using a color property:

```
class Square extends React.Component {
  render() {
    var squareStyle = {
      height: 150,
      backgroundColor: this.props.color
    };

    return (
      <div style={squareStyle}>

      </div>
    );
  }
}

class Label extends React.Component {
  render() {
    var labelStyle = {
      fontFamily: "sans-serif",
      fontWeight: "bold",
      padding: 13,
      margin: 0
    };
```

```
    return (
      <p style={labelStyle}>{this.props.color}</p>
    );
  }
}

class Card extends React.Component {
  render() {
    var cardStyle = {
      height: 200,
      width: 150,
      padding: 0,
      backgroundColor: "#FFF",
      boxShadow: "0px 0px 5px #666"
    };

    return (
      <div style={cardStyle}>
        <Square color={this.props.color} />
        <Label color={this.props.color} />
      </div>
    );
  }
}

ReactDOM.render(
  <div>
    <Card color="#FF6663" />
  </div>,
  document.querySelector("#container")
);
```

After you've made this change, you can specify any hex color you want as part of calling the Card component:

```
ReactDOM.render(
  <div>
    <Card color="#FFA737"/>
  </div>,
  document.querySelector("#container")
);
```

The resulting color palette card features the color you specified (see Figure 5.11).

#FFA737

Figure 5.11   The color for hex value #FFA737.

Now let's go back to the changes we made. Even though the color property is consumed by only the Square and Label components, the parent Card component is responsible for passing the property on to them. For even more deeply nested situations, you'll have more intermediate components that will be responsible for transferring properties. It gets worse. When you have multiple properties that you want to pass around multiple levels of components, the amount of typing (or copying/pasting) you do increases a lot as well. There are ways to mitigate this, and we'll look at those mitigations in much greater detail in a future chapter.

Why Component Composability Rocks

When we're heads-down in React, we often tend to forget that what we are ultimately creating is just plain and boring HTML, CSS, and JavaScript. The generated HTML for our color palette card looks as follows:

```
<div id="container">
  <div>
    <div style="height: 200px;
                width: 150px;
                padding: 0px;
                background-color: rgb(255, 255, 255);
                box-shadow: rgb(102, 102, 102) 0px 0px 5px;">
```

```
            <div style="height: 150px;
                    background-color: rgb(255, 102, 99);">
            </div>
            <p style="font-family: sans-serif;
                    font-weight: bold;
                    padding: 13px;
                    margin: 0px;">
                #FF6663</p>
        </div>
      </div>
</div>
```

This markup has no idea how it got there. It doesn't know about which components were responsible for what. It doesn't care about component composability or the frustrating way we had to transfer the `color` property from parent to child. That brings up an important point to make.

If we had to generalize the end result of what components do, all they do is return blobs of HTML to whatever called it. Each component's `render` function returns some HTML to another component's `render` function. All of this HTML keeps accumulating until a giant blob of HTML is pushed (very efficiently) to our DOM. That simplicity is why component reuse and composability works so well. Each blob of HTML works independently from other blobs of HTML, especially if you specify inline styles as React recommends. This allows you to easily create visual elements from other visual elements without having to worry about anything. *Anything*! Isn't that pretty freaking awesome?

Conclusion

As you might have realized by now, we are slowly shifting focus toward the more advanced scenarios that React thrives in. Actually, *advanced* isn't the right word. The correct word is *realistic*. In this chapter, you started by learning how to look at a piece of UI and identify the components in a way that you can later implement. You'll find yourself in that situation all the time. While the approach we employed seemed really formal, as you get more experienced with creating things in React, you can ratchet down the formality. If you can quickly identify the components and their parent/child relationships without creating a visual and component hierarchy, that's one more sign that you are getting really good at working with React.

Identifying the components is only one part of the equation. The other part is bringing those components to life. Most of the technical stuff you saw here was just a minor extension of what you've already seen. We looked at one level of components in an earlier chapter, and here we looked at how to work with multiple levels of components. We looked at how to pass properties between one parent and one child in an earlier chapter, and here we looked at how to pass properties among multiple parents and multiple children. Maybe in a future chapter we'll do something groundbreaking, like drawing multiple color palette cards to the screen! Or maybe we can specify two properties instead of just a single one. Who knows?

Note: If you run into any issues, ask!

If you have any questions or your code isn't running like you expect, don't hesitate to ask! Post on the forums at https://forum.kirupa.com and get help from some of the friendliest and most knowledgeable people the Internet has ever brought together!

6

Transferring Properties

Working with properties has a frustrating side. We saw a bit of this side in the previous chapter. Passing properties from one component to another is nice and simple when you're dealing with only one layer of components. When you want to send a property across multiple layers of components, things start to get complicated.

Complication is never a good thing, so in this chapter, let's see what we can do to make working with properties easy across multiple layers of components.

Problem Overview

Let's say that you have a deeply nested component, and its hierarchy (modeled as awesomely colored circles) looks like Figure 6.1.

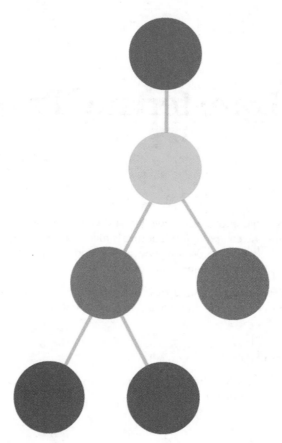

Figure 6.1   The component hierarchy.

You want to pass a property from your red circle all the way down to the purple circles, where it will be used. What you can't do is the very obvious and straightforward thing shown in Figure 6.2.

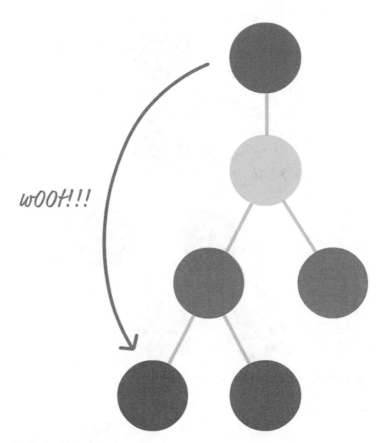

Figure 6.2   Can't do this.

You can't pass a property directly to the component or components that you want to target. The reason has to do with how React works. *React enforces a chain of command in which properties have to flow down from a parent component to an immediate child component.* This means you can't skip a layer of children when sending a property. This also means your children can't send a property back up to a parent. All communication is one-way from the parent to the child.

Under these guidelines, passing a property from our red circle to our purple circle looks a little bit like Figure 6.3.

Every component that lies on the intended path has to receive the property from its parent and then resend that property to its child. This process repeats until your property reaches its intended destination. The problem is in this receiving and resending step.

If we had to send a property called color from the component representing our red circle to the component representing our purple circle, its path to the destination would look something like Figure 6.4.

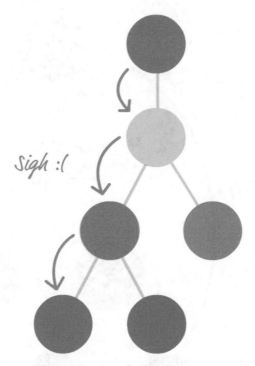

Sigh :(

Figure 6.3   The property is passed from parent to child.

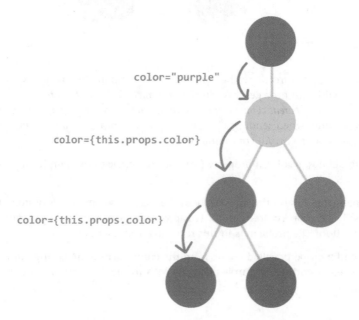

color="purple"

color={this.props.color}

color={this.props.color}

Figure 6.4   Sending the color property.

Now, imagine that we have two properties we need to send, as in Figure 6.5.

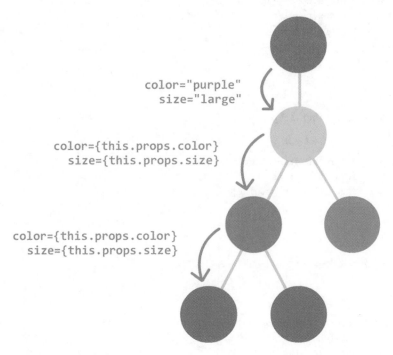

Figure 6.5   Sending two properties.

What if we wanted to send three properties? Or four?

You can see that this approach is neither scalable nor maintainable. For every additional property we need to communicate, we have to add an entry for it as part of declaring each component. If we decide to rename our properties at some point, we have to ensure that every instance of that property is renamed as well. If we remove a property, we need to remove the property from being used across every component that relied on it. Overall, these are the kinds of situations we try to avoid when writing code. What can we do about this?

Detailed Look at the Problem

In the previous section, we talked at a high level about what the problem is. Before we can dive into figuring out a solution, we need to go beyond diagrams and look at a more detailed example with real code. We need to take a look at something like the following:

```
class Display extends React.Component {
  render() {
    return (
```

```
      <div>
        <p>{this.props.color}</p>
        <p>{this.props.num}</p>
        <p>{this.props.size}</p>
      </div>
    );
  }
}

class Label extends React.Component {
  render() {
    return (
      <Display color={this.props.color}
               num={this.props.num}
               size={this.props.size}/>
    );
  }
}

class Shirt extends React.Component {
  render() {
    return (
      <div>
        <Label color={this.props.color}
               num={this.props.num}
               size={this.props.size}/>
      </div>
    );
  }
}

ReactDOM.render(
  <div>
    <Shirt color="steelblue" num="3.14" size="medium" />
  </div>,
  document.querySelector("#container")
);
```

Let's take a few moments to understand what's going on. Then we can walk through this example together.

We have a Shirt component that relies on the output of the Label component, which relies on the output of the Display component. (Try saying that sentence five times fast!) Figure 6.6 shows the component hierarchy.

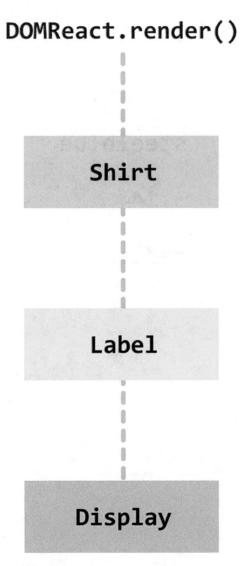

Figure 6.6   The component hierarchy.

When you run this code, the output is nothing special. It's just three lines of text, as shown in Figure 6.7:

Figure 6.7   What our code outputs.

The interesting part is how the text gets there. Each of the three lines of text that you see maps to a property we specified at the very beginning inside ReactDOM.render:

```
<Shirt color="steelblue" num="3.14" size="medium" />
```

The color, num, and size properties (and their values) make a journey all the way to the Display component that would make even the most seasoned world traveler jealous. Let's follow these properties from their inception to when they get consumed. (I realize that a lot of this will be a review of what you've already seen. If you find yourself getting bored, feel free to skip on the next section.)

Life for our properties starts inside ReactDOM.render when our Shirt component gets called with the color, num, and size properties specified:

```
ReactDOM.render(
  <div>
    <Shirt color="steelblue" num="3.14" size="medium" />
  </div>,
  document.querySelector("#container")
);
```

We not only define the properties, but we also initialize them with the values they will carry.

Inside the Shirt component, these properties are stored inside the `props` object. To transfer these properties on, we need to explicitly access these properties from the `props` object and list them as part of the component call. The following is an example of what that looks like when our Shirt component calls our Label component:

```
class Shirt extends React.Component {
  render() {
    return (
      <div>
        <Label color={this.props.color}
               num={this.props.num}
               size={this.props.size} />
      </div>
    );
  }
}
```

Notice that the `color`, `num`, and `size` properties are listed again. The only difference from what we saw with the `ReactDOM.render` call is that the values for each property are taken from their respective entry in the `props` object instead of being manually entered.

When our Label component goes live, it has its `props` object properly filled out with the `color`, `num`, and `size` properties stored. You can probably see a pattern forming here. If you need to let out a big yawn, feel free.

The Label component continues the tradition by repeating the same steps and calling the Display component:

```
class Label extends React.Component {
  render() {
    return (
      <Display color={this.props.color}
               num={this.props.num}
               size={this.props.size} />
    );
  }
}
```

Notice that the Display component call contains the same listing of properties and their values taken from our Label component's `props` object. The only good news from all this is that we're almost done here. The Display component just displays the properties as they were populated inside its `props` object:

```
class Display extends React.Component {
  render() {
    return (
      <div>
        <p>{this.props.color}</p>
        <p>{this.props.num}</p>
```

```
        <p>{this.props.size}</p>
      </div>
    );
  }
}
```

Phew! All we wanted to do was have our Display component display some values for `color`, `num`, and `size`. The only complication was that the values we wanted to display were originally defined as part of `ReactDOM.render`. The annoying solution is the one you see here, with every component along the path to the destination needing to access and redefine each property as part of passing it along. That's just terrible. We can do better than this, and you'll will see how in a few moments.

Meet the Spread Operator

The solution to all our problems lies in something new to JavaScript, known as the **spread operator**. What the spread operator does is a bit bizarre to explain without some context, so let's first give you an example and then bore you with a definition.

Take a look at the following snippet:

```
var items = ["1", "2", "3"];

function printStuff(a, b, c) {
  console.log("Printing: " + a + " " + b + " " + c);
}
```

We have an array called `items` that contains three values. We also have a function called `printStuff` that takes three arguments. We want to specify the three values from our `items` array as arguments to the `printStuff` function. Sounds simple enough, right?

Here's one really common way of doing that:

```
printStuff(items[0], items[1], items[2]);
```

We access each array item individually and pass it in to our `printStuff` function. With the spread operator, we now have an easier way. You don't have to specify each item in the array individually; you can just do something like this:

```
printStuff(...items);
```

The spread operator is the `. . .` characters before our `items` array. Using `...items` is identical to calling `items[0]`, `items[1]`, and `items[2]` individually, as we did earlier. The `printStuff` function will run and print the numbers 1, 2, and 3 to our console. Pretty cool, right?

Now that you've seen the spread operator in action, it's time to define it. *The spread operator allows you to unwrap an array into its individual elements.* The spread operator does a few more things as well, but that's not important for now. We're going to use only this particular side of the spread operator to solve our property transfer problem.

A Better Way to Transfer Properties

You just saw an example of using the spread operator to avoid having to enumerate every single item in our array as part of passing it to a function:

```
var items = ["1", "2", "3"];

function printStuff(a, b, c) {
  console.log("Printing: " + a + " " + b + " " + c);
}

// using the spread operator
printStuff(...items);

// without using the spread operator
printStuff(items[0], items[1], items[2]);
```

The situation we face in transferring properties across components is very similar to our problem of accessing each array item individually. Allow me to elaborate.

Inside a component, our `props` object looks as follows:

```
var props = {
  color: "steelblue",
  num: "3.14",
  size: "medium"
};
```

As part of passing these property values to a child component, we manually access each item from our `props` object:

```
<Display color={this.props.color}
         num={this.props.num}
         size={this.props.size}/>
```

Wouldn't it be great if there was a way to unwrap an object and pass on the property/value pairs just like we were able to unwrap an array using the spread operator?

As it turns out, there is a way. It actually involves the spread operator as well. We explain how later, but this means that we can call our Display component by using ...this.props:

```
<Display {...this.props} />
```

The runtime behavior when using ...this.props is the same as when specifying the color, num, and size properties manually. This means our earlier example can be simplified as follows (pay attention to the highlighted lines):

```
class Display extends React.Component {
  render() {
    return (
```

```
      <div>
        <p>{this.props.color}</p>
        <p>{this.props.num}</p>
        <p>{this.props.size}</p>
      </div>
    );
  }
}

class Label extends React.Component {
  render() {
    return (
      <Display {...this.props} />
    );
  }
}

class Shirt extends React.Component {
  render() {
    return (
      <div>
        <Label {...this.props} />
      </div>
    );
  }
}
```

If you run this code, the end result is unchanged from what we had earlier. The biggest difference is that we are no longer passing in expanded forms of each property as part of calling each component. This solves all the problems we originally set out to solve.

By using the spread operator, if you ever decide to add properties, rename properties, remove properties, or do any other sort of property-related shenanigans, you don't have to make a billion different changes. You make one change at the spot you define your property. You make another change at the spot you consume the property. That's it. All the intermediate components that merely transfer the properties remain untouched because the {...this.props} expression contains no details of what goes on inside it.

Is this the best way to transfer properties?

Using the spread operator to transfer properties is convenient, and it's a marked improvement over explicitly defining each property at each component as we were originally doing. The thing is, even the spread operator approach isn't a perfect solution. If all you want to do is transfer a property to a particular component, having each intermediate component play a role in passing it on is unnecessary. Worse, it has the potential to be a performance bottleneck. Any change to a property that you are passing along will trigger a component update on each component along the property's path. That's not a good thing! Later, we look at ways to solve this transferring properties problem in a much better, without any side effects.

Conclusion

As created by the ES6/ES2015 committee, the spread operator is designed to work only on arrays and arraylike creatures (a.k.a. something that has a `Symbol.iterator` property). The fact that it works on object literals such as our `props` object is a result of React extending the standard. No browser currently supports using the spread object on object literals. Our example works because of Babel. Besides turning all our JSX into something our browser understands, Babel turns cutting-edge and experimental features into something that's friendly across browsers. That's why we're able to get away with using the spread operator on an object literal, and that's why we're able to elegantly solve the problem of transferring properties across multiple layers of components.

Now, does any of this matter? Is it really critical that you know about the nuances of the spread operator and how it works in certain situations and doesn't work in others? For the most part, no. The important part to realize is that you can use the spread operator to transfer `props` from one component to another. The other important part to realize is that we will look at some other ways in the future to make transferring properties equally simple, without running into any performance issues.

Note: If you run into any issues, ask!

If you have any questions or your code isn't running like you expect, don't hesitate to ask! Post on the forums at https://forum.kirupa.com and get help from some of the friendliest and most knowledgeable people the Internet has ever brought together!

7

Meet JSX...Again!

As you've probably noticed by now, we've been using a lot of JSX. But we really haven't taken a good look at what JSX actually is. How does it work? Why don't we just call it HTML? What quirks does it have up its sleeve? In this chapter, we answer all those questions and more! We do some serious backtracking (and some forwardtracking) to see what we need to know about JSX in order to be dangerous.

What Happens with JSX?

One of the biggest things we've glossed over is trying to figure out what happens with our JSX after we've written it. How does it end up as the HTML that you see in the browser? Take a look at the following example, where we define a component called `Card`:

```
class Card extends React.Component {
  render() {
    var cardStyle = {
      height: 200,
      width: 150,
      padding: 0,
      backgroundColor: "#FFF",
      boxShadow: "0px 0px 5px #666"
    };

    return (
      <div style={cardStyle}>
        <Square color={this.props.color} />
        <Label color={this.props.color} />
      </div>
    );
  }
}
```

We can quickly spot the JSX here. It's the following four lines:

```
<div style={cardStyle}>
  <Square color={this.props.color} />
  <Label color={this.props.color} />
</div>
```

Keep in mind that browsers have no idea what to do with JSX. They probably think you're crazy if you even try to describe JSX to them. That's why we've been relying on things like Babel to turn that JSX into something the browsers understand: JavaScript.

This means that the JSX we write is for human (and well-trained cat) eyes only. When this JSX reaches our browser, it ends up getting turned into pure JavaScript:

```
return React.createElement(
  "div",
  { style: cardStyle },
  React.createElement(Square, { color: this.props.color }),
  React.createElement(Label, { color: this.props.color })
);
```

All of those neatly nested HTML-like elements, their attributes, and their children get turned into a series of `createElement` calls with default initialization values. Here's what our entire Card component looks like when it gets turned into JavaScript:

```
class Card extends React.Component {
  render() {
    var cardStyle = {
      height: 200,
      width: 150,
      padding: 0,
      backgroundColor: "#FFF",
      boxShadow: "0px 0px 5px #666"
    };

    return React.createElement(
      "div",
      { style: cardStyle },
      React.createElement(Square, { color: this.props.color }),
      React.createElement(Label, { color: this.props.color })
    );
  }
}
```

Notice that there's no trace of JSX anywhere! All these changes between what we wrote and what our browser sees are part of the transpiling step we talked about in Chapter 1, "Introducing React." That transpilation happens entirely behind the scenes, thanks to Babel, which we've been using to perform this JSX-to-JS transformation entirely in the browser. We'll eventually look at using Babel as part of a more involved build environment in which we generate a transformed JS file, but you'll see more on that when we get there in the future.

So there you have it, an answer to what exactly happens to all our JSX: It gets turned into *sweet* JavaScript.

JSX Quirks to Remember

As we've been working with JSX, you've probably noticed that we've run into some arbitrary rules and exceptions on what we can and can't do. In this section, let's look at those quirks...and some brand new ones!

Evaluating Expressions

JSX is treated like JavaScript. As you've seen a few times already, this means that you aren't limited to dealing with static content like the following:

```
class Stuff extends React.Component {
  render() {
    return (
      <h1>Boring static content!</h1>
    );
  }
};
```

The values you return can be dynamically generated. All you have to do is wrap your expression in curly braces:

```
class Stuff extends React.Component {
  render() {
    return (
      <h1>Boring {Math.random() * 100} content!</h1>
    );
  }
}
```

Notice that we're throwing in a `Math.random()` call to generate a random number. It gets evaluated along with the static text alongside it, but because of the curly braces, what you see looks something like the following: *Boring 28.6388820148227 content!*

These curly braces allow your app to first evaluate the expression and then return the result of the evaluation. Without them, you would see your expression returned as text: *Boring Math.random() * 100 content!*

That isn't what you would probably want.

Returning Multiple Elements

In a lot of our examples, we've returned one top-level element (often a `div`) that then had many other elements under it. You aren't technically limited to following that pattern: You can actually return multiple elements. And you can do that in two ways.

One way is to use an arraylike syntax:

```
class Stuff extends React.Component {
  render() {
    return (
      [
        <p>I am</p>,
        <p>returning a list</p>,
        <p>of things!</p>
      ]
    );
  }
}
```

Here we are returning three `p` tags. They don't have a single common parent. Now, when you return multiple items, you might or might not have to deal with one detail, depending on the version of React you are targeting. You need to specify a `key` attribute and a unique value for each item:

```
class Stuff extends React.Component {
  render() {
    return (
      [
        <p key="1">I am</p>,
        <p key="2">returning a list</p>,
        <p key="3">of things!</p>
      ]
    );
  }
}
```

This helps React better understand which element it is dealing with and whether to make any changes to it. How do you know whether you need to add the `key` attribute? React tells you. You'll see a message similar to the following printed to your Dev Tools Console: *Warning: Each child in an array or iterator should have a unique "key" prop.*

You also have another (and, arguably, better) way to return multiple elements. This involves something known as fragments. The way you use it looks as follows:

```
class Stuff extends React.Component {
  render() {
    return (
      <React.Fragment>
        <p>I am</p>
```

```
          <p>returning a list</p>
          <p>of things!</p>
        </React.Fragment>
    );
  }
}
```

You wrap the list of items you want to return into a magical `React.Fragment` component. Note a few cool things here:

1. This component doesn't actually generate a DOM element. It is just something you specify in JSX that has no tangible existence when transpiled into the HTML your browser sees.

2. You aren't treating what you are returning as items in an array, so you don't need commas or anything separating each item.

3. There's no need to specify a unique key attribute and value; this is all taken care of under the covers for you.

Before we leave this section, know that you can use a more condensed syntax instead of fully specifying `React.Fragment`... like an animal. You can use just empty `<>` and `</>` tags:

```
class Stuff extends React.Component {
  render() {
    return (
      <>
        <p>I am</p>
        <p>returning a list</p>
        <p>of things!</p>
      </>
    );
  }
}
```

This looks like something from the future, so if you're inclined to use fragments to return multiple values, feel free to use this smaller syntax.

You Can't Specify CSS Inline

As you saw in Chapter 4, "Styling in React," the `style` attribute in your JSX behaves differently from the `style` attribute in HTML. In HTML, you can specify CSS properties directly as values on your `style` attribute:

```
<div style="font-family:Arial;font-size:24px">
  <p>Blah!</p>
</div>
```

In JSX, the `style` attribute can't contain CSS inside it. Instead, it needs to refer to an object that contains styling information:

```
class Letter extends React.Component {
  render() {
    var letterStyle = {
      padding: 10,
      margin: 10,
      backgroundColor: this.props.bgcolor,
      color: "#333",
      display: "inline-block",
      fontFamily: "monospace",
      fontSize: "32",
      textAlign: "center"
    };

    return (
      <div style={letterStyle}>
        {this.props.children}
      </div>
    );
  }
}
```

Notice that we have an object called `letterStyle` that that contains all the CSS properties (in camel-case JavaScript form) and their values. That object is what we then specify to the `style` attribute.

Comments

Just as it's a good idea to comment your HTML, CSS, and JavaScript, it's a good idea to provide comments inside your JSX. Specifying comments in JSX is similar to how you comment in JavaScript, with one exception. If you're specifying a comment as a child of a tag, you need to enclose your comment within the { and } angle brackets to ensure that it is parsed as an expression:

```
ReactDOM.render(
  <div className="slideIn">
    <p className="emphasis">Gabagool!</p>
    {/* I am a child comment */}
    <Label/>
  </div>,
  document.querySelector("#container")
);
```

Our comment in this case is a child of our `div` element. If you specify a comment wholly inside a tag, you can just specify your single-line or multiline comment without having to use the { and } angle brackets:

```
ReactDOM.render(
  <div className="slideIn">
    <p className="emphasis">Gabagool!</p>
    <Label
      /* This comment
         goes across
         multiple lines */
         className="colorCard" // end of line
    />
  </div>,
  document.querySelector("#container")
);
```

In this snippet, you can see an example of both a multiline comment and a comment at the end of a line. Now that you know all of this, you have one less excuse to not comment your JSX.

Capitalization, HTML Elements, and Components

Capitalization is important. To represent HTML elements, ensure that the HTML tag is lowercase:

```
ReactDOM.render(
  <div>
    <section>
      <p>Something goes here!</p>
    </section>
  </div>,
  document.querySelector("#container")
);
```

When you want to represent components, the component name must be capitalized:

```
ReactDOM.render(
  <div>
    <MyCustomComponent/>
  </div>,
  document.querySelector("#container")
);
```

If you get the capitalization wrong, React will not render your content properly. Trying to identify capitalization issues is probably the last point you'll think about when things aren't working, so keep this little tip in mind.

Your JSX Can Be Anywhere

In many situations, your JSX won't be neatly arranged inside a `render` or `return` function as in the examples you've seen so far. Take a look at the following example:

```
var swatchComponent = <Swatch color="#2F004F"></Swatch>;

ReactDOM.render(
  <div>
    {swatchComponent}
  </div>,
  document.querySelector("#container")
);
```

We have a variable called `swatchComponent` that is initialized to a line of JSX. When our `swatchComponent` variable is placed inside the `render` function, our Swatch component gets initialized. All of this is totally valid. You will do more such things in the future when you learn how to generate and manipulate JSX using JavaScript.

Conclusion

With this chapter, we've finally pieced together in one location the various bits of JSX information that the previous chapters introduced. The most important point to remember is that *JSX is not HTML*. It looks like HTML and behaves like it in many common scenarios, but it is ultimately designed to be translated into JavaScript. This means you can do things that you could never imagine doing using just plain HTML. Being able to evaluate expressions or programmatically manipulate entire chunks of JSX is just the beginning. In upcoming chapters, we'll explore this intersection of JavaScript and JSX further.

> **Note: If you run into any issues, ask!**
>
> If you have any questions or your code isn't running like you expect, don't hesitate to ask! Post on the forums at https://forum.kirupa.com and get help from some of the friendliest and most knowledgeable people the Internet has ever brought together!

8

Dealing with State in React

Up to this point, the components we've created have been stateless. They have properties (a.k.a. `props`) that are passed in from their parent, but nothing (usually) changes about them once the components come alive. Your properties are considered immutable once they've been set. For many interactive scenarios, you don't want that. You want to be able to change aspects of your components as a result of some user interaction (or some data getting returned from a server or a billion other things).

We need another way to store data on a component that goes beyond properties. We need a way to store data that can be changed. What we need is something known as **state**. In this chapter, you learn all about state and how you can use it to create stateful components.

Using State

If you know how to work with properties, you totally know how to work with states...sort of. There are some differences, but they're too subtle to bore you with right now. Instead, let's just jump right in and see states in action by using them in a small example.

We're going to create a simple lightning counter example, as shown in Figure 8.1.

Figure 8.1   The app you will be building.

This example does nothing crazy. Lightning strikes Earth's surface about 100 times a second, according to *National Geographic*. We have a counter that simply increments a number you see by that same amount. Let's create it.

Our Starting Point

The primary focus of this example is to see how we can work with state. There's no point spending a lot of time creating the example from scratch and retracing paths that we've walked many times already. That's not the best use of anybody's time.

Instead of starting from scratch, modify an existing HTML document or create a new one with the following contents:

```
<!DOCTYPE html>
<html>

<head>
  <meta charset="utf-8">
  <title>Dealing with State</title>
  <script src="https://unpkg.com/react@16/umd/react.development.js"></script>
```

```html
    <script src="https://unpkg.com/react-dom@16/umd/react-dom.development.js"></script>
    <script src="https://unpkg.com/babel-standalone@6.15.0/babel.min.js"></script>
</head>

<body>
  <div id="container"></div>

  <script type="text/babel">
    class LightningCounter extends React.Component {
      render() {
        return (
          <h1>Hello!</h1>
        );
      }
    }

    class LightningCounterDisplay extends React.Component {
      render() {
        var divStyle = {
          width: 250,
          textAlign: "center",
          backgroundColor: "black",
          padding: 40,
          fontFamily: "sans-serif",
          color: "#999",
          borderRadius: 10
        };

        return (
          <div style={divStyle}>
            <LightningCounter/>
          </div>
        );
      }
    }

    ReactDOM.render(
      <LightningCounterDisplay/>,
      document.querySelector("#container")
    );
  </script>
</body>

</html>
```

Now let's take a few minutes to look at what our existing code does. First, we have a component called `LightningCounterDisplay`. The bulk of this component is the `divStyle` object, which contains the styling information responsible for the cool rounded background. The `return` function returns a `div` element that wraps the `LightningCounter` component.

The `LightningCounter` component is where all the action will take place:

```
class LightningCounter extends React.Component {
  render() {
    return (
      <h1>Hello!</h1>
    );
  }
}
```

As it is right now, this component has nothing interesting going for it. It just returns the word **Hello!** That's okay—we'll fix up this component later.

The last thing to look at is our `ReactDOM.render` method:

```
ReactDOM.render(
  <LightningCounterDisplay/>,
  document.querySelector("#container")
);
```

It just pushes the `LightningCounterDisplay` component to our `container` element in our DOM. That's pretty much it. The end result is the combination of markup from our `ReactDOM.render` method and the `LightningCounterDisplay` and `LightningCounter` components.

Getting Our Counter On

Now that you have an idea of what we're starting with, it's time to make plans for our next steps. The way our counter works is pretty simple. We're going to be using a `setInterval` function that calls some code every 1000 milliseconds (a.k.a. 1 second). That "some code" is going to increment a value by 100 each time it's called. Seems pretty straightforward, right?

To make this all work, we're relying on three APIs that our React component exposes:

1. `componentDidMount`

   This method gets called just *after* our component gets rendered (or **mounted**, as React calls it).

2. `setState`

   This method allows you to update the value of the `state` object.

You'll see these APIs in use shortly, but here you get a preview so that you can spot them easily in a lineup.

Setting the Initial State Value

We need a variable to act as our counter. Let's call this variable `strikes`. We have a bunch of ways to create this variable, but the most obvious one is the following:

```
var strikes = 0; // :P
```

We don't want to do that, though. For our example, the `strikes` variable is part of our component's state. We want to create a `state` object, make our `strikes` variable a property of it, and ensure that we set all of this up when our component is getting created. The component we want to do all this to is `LightningCounter`. Go ahead and add the following highlighted lines:

```
class LightningCounter extends React.Component {
  constructor(props) {
    super(props);

    this.state = {
      strikes: 0
    };
  }

  render() {
    return (
      <h1>Hello!</h1>
    );
  }
}
```

We specify our `state` object inside our `LightningCounter` component's constructor. This runs way before your component gets rendered. We're telling React to set an object containing our `strikes` property (initialized to **0**).

If we inspect the value of our state object after this code has run, it looks something like the following:

```
var state = {
  strikes: 0
};
```

Before we wrap up this section up, let's visualize our `strikes` property. In our `render` method, make the following highlighted change:

```
class LightningCounter extends React.Component {
  constructor(props) {
    super(props);

    this.state = {
      strikes: 0
    };
  }
```

```
render() {
  return (
    <h1>{this.state.strikes}</h1>
  );
}
}
```

We've replaced our default **Hello!** text with an expression that displays the value stored by the this.state.strikes property. If you preview your example in the browser, you will see a value of **0** displayed. That's a start!

Starting Our Timer and Setting State

Next up, is getting our timer going and incrementing our strikes property. As we mentioned earlier, we will be using the setInterval function to increase the strikes property by 100 every second. We're going to do all of this immediately after our component has been rendered using the built-in componentDidMount method.

The code for kicking off our timer looks as follows:

```
class LightningCounter extends React.Component {
  constructor(props) {
    super(props);

    this.state = {
      strikes: 0
    };
  }

  timerTick() {
    this.setState({
      strikes: this.state.strikes + 100
    });
  }

  componentDidMount() {
    setInterval(this.timerTick, 1000);
  }

  render() {
    return (
      <h1>{this.state.strikes}</h1>
    );
  }
}
```

Go ahead and add these highlighted lines to our example. Inside our `componentDidMount` method that gets called after our component gets rendered, we have our `setInterval` method that calls a `timerTick` function every second (or 1000 milliseconds).

We haven't defined our `timerTick` function, so let's fix that by adding the following highlighted lines to our code:

```
class LightningCounter extends React.Component {
  constructor(props) {
    super(props);

    this.state = {
      strikes: 0
    };
  }

  timerTick() {
    this.setState({
      strikes: this.state.strikes + 100
    });
  }

  componentDidMount() {
    setInterval(this.timerTick, 1000);
  }

  render() {
    return (
      <h1>{this.state.strikes}</h1>
    );
  }
}
```

What our `timerTick` function does is pretty simple: It just calls `setState`. The `setState` method comes in various flavors, but for what we're doing here, it just takes an object as its argument. This object contains all the properties you want to *merge into the* `state` *object*. In our case, we are specifying the `strikes` property and setting its value to be 100 more than what it is currently.

Note: Incrementing the Existing State Value

As you've seen here, you will often end up modifying an existing state value with an updated value. We're getting the existing state value by calling `this.state.strikes`. For performance-related reasons, React might decide to batch state updates in rapid succession. This could lead to the original value stored by `this.state` to be out-of-sync with reality. To help with this, the `setState` method gives you access to the previous state object via the `prevState` argument.

Using that argument, our code could be made to look as follows:

```
this.setState((prevState) => {
  return {
    strikes: prevState.strikes + 100
  };
});
```

The end result is similar to what we had originally. Our `strikes` property is incremented by 100. The only potential change is that the value of the `strikes` property is guaranteed to be whatever the earlier value stored by our state object would be.

So should you use this approach to update your state? There are good arguments on both sides. One side argues for correctness, despite `this.state` working out fine for most real-world cases. The other side argues for keeping the code simple and not introducing additional complexity. There's no right or wrong answer here, so use whatever approach you prefer. I'm calling this out only for completeness because you could run into the `prevState` approach in any React code you encounter in the wild.

You need to do one more thing. The `timerTick` function has been added to our component, but *its contents* don't have their context set to our component. In other words, the `this` keyword where we are accessing `setState` will return a `TypeError` in the current situation. You can employ several solutions here, each a little frustrating in its own way. We'll look at this problem in detail later. For now, we're going to explicitly bind our `timerTick` function to our component so that all the `this` references resolve properly. Add the following line to our constructor:

```
constructor(props) {
    super(props);

    this.state = {
        strikes: 0
    };

    this.timerTick = this.timerTick.bind(this);
}
```

When you've done this, the `timerTick` function is ready to be a useful part of our component.

Rendering the State Change

If you preview your app now, you'll see our `strikes` value start to increment by 100 every second (see Figure 8.2).

Figure 8.2   The `strikes` value increments by 100 every second.

Let's ignore for a moment what happens with our code. That's pretty straightforward. The interesting thing is that everything we've done ends up updating what you see onscreen. That updating has to do with this React behavior: *Whenever you call setState and update something in the state object, your component's render method gets automatically called.* This kicks off a cascade of `render` calls for any component whose output is also affected. The end result of all this is that what you see on your screen in the latest representation of your app's UI state. Keeping your data and UI in sync is one of the hardest problems with UI development, so it's nice that React takes care of this for us. It makes all this pain of learning to use React totally worth it...almost!

Optional: The Full Code

What we have right now is just a counter that increments by 100 every second. Nothing about it screams **lightning counter**, but it does cover everything about states that I wanted you to learn right now. If you want to optionally flesh out your example to look like our version that you saw at the beginning, this is the full code for what goes inside our script tag:

```
class LightningCounter extends React.Component {
  constructor(props) {
    super(props);

    this.state = {
      strikes: 0
    };

    this.timerTick = this.timerTick.bind(this);
  }
```

```
  timerTick() {
    this.setState({
      strikes: this.state.strikes + 100
    });
  }

  componentDidMount() {
    setInterval(this.timerTick, 1000);
  }

  render() {
    var counterStyle = {
      color: "#66FFFF",
      fontSize: 50
    };

    var count = this.state.strikes.toLocaleString();

    return (
      <h1 style={counterStyle}>{count}</h1>
    );
  }
}

class LightningCounterDisplay extends React.Component {
  render() {
    var commonStyle = {
      margin: 0,
      padding: 0
    };

    var divStyle = {
      width: 250,
      textAlign: "center",
      backgroundColor: "#020202",
      padding: 40,
      fontFamily: "sans-serif",
      color: "#999999",
      borderRadius: 10
    };

    var textStyles = {
      emphasis: {
        fontSize: 38,
        ...commonStyle
      },
```

```
      smallEmphasis: {
        ...commonStyle
      },
      small: {
        fontSize: 17,
        opacity: 0.5,
        ...commonStyle
      }
    };

    return (
      <div style={divStyle}>
        <LightningCounter />
        <h2 style={textStyles.smallEmphasis}>LIGHTNING STRIKES</h2>
        <h2 style={textStyles.emphasis}>WORLDWIDE</h2>
        <p style={textStyles.small}>(since you loaded this example)</p>
      </div>
    );
  }
}

ReactDOM.render(
  <LightningCounterDisplay />,
  document.querySelector("#container")
);
```

If you make your code look like everything you see here and run the example again, you will see our lightning counter example in all its cyan-colored glory. While you're at it, take a moment to look through the code to ensure that you don't see too many surprises.

Conclusion

We just scratched the surface on what we can do to create stateful components. While using a timer to update something in our state object is cool, the real action happens when we start combining user interaction with state. So far, we've shied away from the large amount of mouse, touch, keyboard, and other related things that your components will come into contact with. In an upcoming chapter, we fix that. Along the way, you'll see us taking what we've seen about states to a whole new level. If that doesn't excite you, then I don't know what will.

> ### Note: If you run into any issues, ask!
>
> If you have any questions or your code isn't running like you expect, don't hesitate to ask! Post on the forums at https://forum.kirupa.com and get help from some of the friendliest and most knowledgeable people the Internet has ever brought together!

9

Going from Data to UI in React

When you're building your apps, thinking in terms of props, state, components, JSX tags, render methods, and other React-isms might be the last thing on your mind. Most of the time, you're dealing with data in the form of JSON objects, arrays, and other data structures that have no knowledge (or interest) in React or anything visual. Bridging the gulf between your data and what you eventually see can be frustrating! Not to worry, though. This chapter helps reduce some of those frustrating moments by running through some common scenarios you'll encounter.

The Example

To help make sense of everything you're about to see, we need an example. It's nothing too complicated, so go ahead and create a new HTML document and throw the following stuff into it:

```html
<!DOCTYPE html>
<html>

<head>
  <meta charset="utf-8">
  <title>From Data to UI</title>
  <script src="https://unpkg.com/react@16/umd/react.development.js"></script>
  <script src="https://unpkg.com/react-dom@16/umd/react-dom.development.js"></script>
  <script src="https://unpkg.com/babel-standalone@6.15.0/babel.min.js"></script>

  <style>
    #container {
      padding: 50px;
      background-color: #FFF;
    }
  </style>
</head>
```

```
<body>
  <div id="container"></div>

  <script type="text/babel">
    class Circle extends React.Component {
      render() {
        var circleStyle = {
          padding: 10,
          margin: 20,
          display: "inline-block",
          backgroundColor: this.props.bgColor,
          borderRadius: "50%",
          width: 100,
          height: 100,
        };

        return (
          <div style={circleStyle}>
          </div>
        );
      }
    }

    ReactDOM.render(
      <div>
        <Circle bgColor="#F9C240" />
      </div>,
      document.querySelector("#container");
    );
  </script>
</body>

</html>
```

When you have your document set up, go ahead and preview what you have in your browser. If everything went well, you'll be greeted by a happy yellow circle (see Figure 9.1).

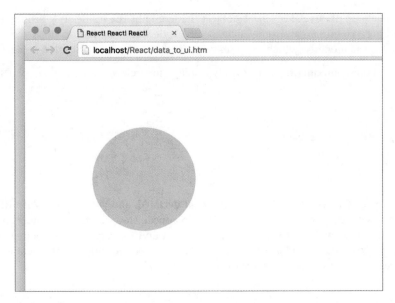

Figure 9.1   If everything went well, you'll get this yellow circle.

If you see what I see, great! Now, let's take a moment to understand what this example is doing. The bulk of what you see comes from the Circle component:

```
class Circle extends React.Component {
  render() {
    var circleStyle = {
      padding: 10,
      margin: 20,
      display: "inline-block",
      backgroundColor: this.props.bgColor,
      borderRadius: "50%",
      width: 100,
      height: 100,
    };

    return (
      <div style={circleStyle}>
      </div>
    );
  }
}
```

It's mostly made up of our `circleStyle` object that contains the inline style properties that turn our boring `div` into an awesome circle. All the style values are hard-coded except for the `backgroundColor` property, which takes its value from the `bgColor` prop that gets passed in.

Going beyond our component, we ultimately display our circle via our usual `ReactDOM.render` method:

```
ReactDOM.render(
  <div>
    <Circle bgColor="#F9C240"/>
  </div>,
  destination
);
```

We have a single instance of our Circle component declared, and we declare it with the `bgColor` prop set to the color we want our circle to appear. Now, having our Circle component be defined as is inside our `render` method is a bit limiting, especially if we're going to be dealing with data that could affect what our Circle component does. In the next couple sections, we'll look at the ways we have for solving that.

Your JSX Can Be Anywhere, Part II

In Chapter 7, "Meet JSX...Again" , you learned that JSX can actually live outside a `render` function and can be used as a value assigned to a variable or property. For example, we can fearlessly do something like this:

```
var theCircle = <Circle bgColor="#F9C240" />;

ReactDOM.render(
  <div>
    {theCircle}
  </div>,
  destination
);
```

The `theCircle` variable stores the JSX for instantiating our Circle component. Evaluating this variable inside our `ReactDOM.render` function results in a circle getting displayed. The end result is no different than what we had earlier, but freeing our Circle component instantiation from the shackles of the `render` method gives us more options to do crazy and cool things.

For example, you can go further and create a function that returns a Circle component:

```
function showCircle() {
  var colors = ["#393E41", "#E94F37", "#1C89BF", "#A1D363"];
  var ran = Math.floor(Math.random() * colors.length);

  // return a Circle with a randomly chosen color
  return <Circle bgColor={colors[ran]} />;
}
```

In this case, the `showCircle` function returns a Circle component (boring!) with the value for the `bgColor` prop set to a random color value (awesome sauce!). To have our example use the `showCircle` function, all you have to do is evaluate it inside `ReactDOM.render`:

```
ReactDOM.render(
  <div>
    {showCircle()}
  </div>,
  destination
);
```

As long as the expression you're evaluating returns JSX, you can put pretty much anything you want inside the { and } brackets. That flexibility is really nice because you can do *a lot* when your JavaScript lives outside the `render` function.

Dealing with Arrays

Now we get to some fun stuff! When you're displaying multiple components, you can't always manually specify them:

```
ReactDOM.render(
  <div>
    {showCircle()}
    {showCircle()}
    {showCircle()}
  </div>,
  destination
);
```

In many real-world scenarios, the number of components you display is related to the number of items in an array or arraylike (a.k.a. iterator) object you're working with. That brings up a few simple complications. For example, let's say that we have an array called `colors` that looks as follows:

```
var colors = ["#393E41", "#E94F37", "#1C89BF", "#A1D363",
              "#85FFC7", "#297373", "#FF8552", "#A40E4C"];
```

We want to create a Circle component for each item in this array (and set the `bgColor` prop to the value of each array item). We can do this by creating an array of Circle components:

```
var colors = ["#393E41", "#E94F37", "#1C89BF", "#A1D363",
              "#85FFC7", "#297373", "#FF8552", "#A40E4C"];

var renderData = [];

for (var i = 0; i < colors.length; i++) {
  renderData.push(<Circle bgColor={colors[i]} />);
}
```

In this snippet, we populate our `renderData` array with Circle components just as we originally set out to do. So far, so good. React makes displaying all of these components very simple. Take a look at the highlighted line for all you have to do:

```
ReactDOM.render(
  <div>
    {renderData}
  </div>,
  destination
);
```

In our `render` method, all we do is specify our `renderData` array as an expression that we need to evaluate. We don't need to take any other step to go from an array of components to something that looks like Figure 9.2 when you preview in your browser.

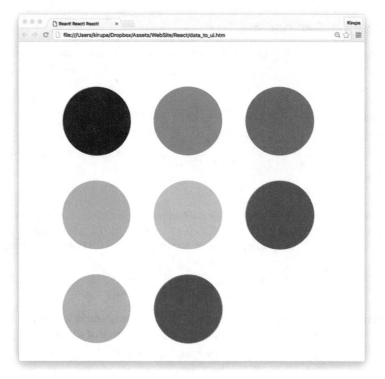

Figure 9.2 What you should see in your browser.

Okay, I lied. There's actually one more thing we need to do, and it's a subtle one. React makes UI updates really fast by having a good idea of what exactly is going on in your DOM. It does this in several ways, but one really noticeable way is by internally marking each element with some sort of an identifier.

When you create elements dynamically (such as what we're doing with our array of Circle components), these identifiers are not automatically set. We need to do some extra work. That extra work takes the form of a key prop whose value React uses to uniquely identify each particular component.

For our example, we can do something like this:

```
for (var i = 0; i < colors.length; i++) {
  var color = colors[i];
  renderData.push(<Circle key={i + color} bgColor={color} />);
}
```

On each component, we specify our key prop and set its value to a combination of color and index position inside the colors array. This ensures that each component we dynamically create ends up getting a unique identifier that React can then use to optimize any future UI updates.

Check Your Console, Yo!

React is really good at telling you when you might be doing something wrong. For example, if you dynamically create elements or components and don't specify a key prop on them, you'll be greeted with the following warning in your console:

```
Warning: Each child in an array or iterator should have a unique "key" prop.
Check the top-level render call using <div>.
```

When you're working with React, it's a good idea to periodically check your console for any messages. Even if things seem to be working just fine, you never know what you might find.

Conclusion

All the tips and tricks you've seen in this article are made possible because of one thing: *JSX is JavaScript.* This is what allows you to have your JSX live wherever JavaScript thrives. To us, it looks like we're doing something absolutely bizarre when we specify something like this:

```
for (var i = 0; i < colors.length; i++) {
  var color = colors[i];
  renderData.push(<Circle key={i + color} bgColor={color} />);
}
```

Even though we're pushing pieces of JSX to an array, just like magic, everything works in the end when `renderData` is evaluated inside our `render` method. I hate to sound like a broken record, but this is because what our browser ultimately sees looks like this:

```
for (var i = 0; i < colors.length; i++) {
  var color = colors[i];

  renderData.push(React.createElement(Circle,
    {
      key: i + color,
      bgColor: color
    }));
}
```

When our JSX gets converted into pure JS, everything makes sense again. This is what allows us to get away with putting our JSX in all sorts of uncomfortable (yet photogenic!) situations and still get the end result we want. In the end, it's all just JavaScript.

Note: If you run into any issues, ask!

If you have any questions or your code isn't running like you expect, don't hesitate to ask! Post on the forums at https://forum.kirupa.com and get help from some of the friendliest and most knowledgeable people the Internet has ever brought together!

10

Events in React

So far, most of our examples did their work only upon page load. As you probably guessed, that isn't normal. In most apps, especially the kind of UI-heavy ones you'll be building, the app will do a ton of things only as a reaction to something. Those *somethings* could be triggered by a mouse click, a key press, a window resize, or a whole bunch of other gestures and interactions. **Events** are the glue that makes all of this possible.

Now, you probably know all about events from your experience using them in the DOM world. (If you don't, then I suggest getting a quick refresher first: https://www.kirupa.com/html5/ javascript_events.htm.) The way React deals with events is a bit different, and these differences can surprise you if you aren't paying close attention. Don't worry, that's why you have this book! We start off with a few simple examples and then gradually look at increasingly more bizarre, complex, and (yes!) boring things.

Listening and Reacting to Events

The easiest way to learn about events in React is to actually use them, and that's exactly what you're going to do here. To help with this, we have a simple example made up of a counter that increments each time you click a button. Initially, our example will look like Figure 10.1.

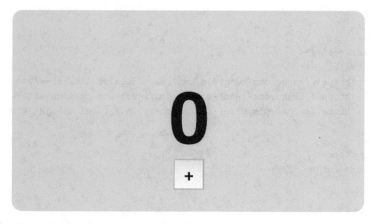

Figure 10.1   Our example.

Each time you click the plus button, the counter value will increase by 1. After you click the plus button a bunch of times, it will look sort of like Figure 10.2.

Figure 10.2   After clicking the plus button a bunch of times (23).

Under the covers, this example is pretty simple. Each time you click on the button, an event gets fired. We listen for this event and do all sorts of React-ey things to get the counter to update when this event gets overheard.

Starting Point

To save all of us some time, we aren't going to be creating everything in our example from scratch. By now, you probably have a good idea of how to work with components, styles, state, and so on. Instead, we're going to start off with a partially implemented example that contains everything except the event-related functionality that you're here to learn.

First, create a new HTML document and ensure that your starting point looks as follows:

```
<!DOCTYPE html>
<html>

<head>
  <meta charset="utf-8">
  <title>Events</title>
  <script src="https://unpkg.com/react@16/umd/react.development.js"></script>
  <script src="https://unpkg.com/react-dom@16/umd/react-dom.development.js"></script>
  <script src="https://unpkg.com/babel-standalone@6.15.0/babel.min.js"></script>
  <style>
    #container {
      padding: 50px;
      background-color: #FFF;
    }
  </style>
</head>
```

```
<body>
  <div id="container"></div>
  <script type="text/babel">

  </script>
</body>

</html>
```

When your new HTML document looks like what you see, it's time to add our partially implemented counter example. Inside our `script` tag below the `container` div, add the following:

```
class Counter extends React.Component {
  render() {
    var textStyle = {
      fontSize: 72,
      fontFamily: "sans-serif",
      color: "#333",
      fontWeight: "bold"
    };

    return (
      <div style={textStyle}>
        {this.props.display}
      </div>
    );
  }
}

class CounterParent extends React.Component {
  constructor(props) {
    super(props);

    this.state = {
      count: 0
    };
  }

  render() {
    var backgroundStyle = {
      padding: 50,
      backgroundColor: "#FFC53A",
      width: 250,
      height: 100,
      borderRadius: 10,
      textAlign: "center"
    };
```

```
    var buttonStyle = {
      fontSize: "1em",
      width: 30,
      height: 30,
      fontFamily: "sans-serif",
      color: "#333",
      fontWeight: "bold",
      lineHeight: "3px"
    };

    return (
      <div style={backgroundStyle}>
        <Counter display={this.state.count} />
        <button style={buttonStyle}>+</button>
      </div>
    );
  }
}


ReactDOM.render(
  <div>
    <CounterParent />
  </div>,
  document.querySelector("#container")
);
```

Now preview everything in your browser to make sure it works. You should see the beginning of our counter. Take a few moments to look at what all of this code does. You shouldn't
see anything that looks strange. The only odd thing is that clicking the plus button won't do
anything. We'll fix that in the next section.

Making the Button Click Do Something

Each time we click the plus button, we want the value of our counter to increase by 1. What we
need to do roughly looks like this:

1. Listen for the click event on the button.

2. Implement the event handler so that we react to the click and increase the value of our
    `this.state.count` property that our counter relies on.

We'll just go straight down the list, starting with listening for the click event. In React, you
listen to an event by specifying everything inline in your JSX itself. More specifically, *you specify
inside your markup both the event you're listening for and the event handler that will get called.* To do

this, find the return function inside our `CounterParent` component and make the following highlighted change:

```
   .
   .
   .

return (
  <div style={backgroundStyle}>
    <Counter display={this.state.count}/>
    <button onClick={this.increase} style={buttonStyle}>+</button>
  </div>
);
```

We've told React to call the `increase` function when the `onClick` event is overheard. Next, let's go ahead and implement the `increase` function (a.k.a. our event handler). Inside our `CounterParent` component, add the following highlighted lines:

```
class CounterParent extends React.Component {
  constructor(props) {
    super(props);

    this.state = {
      count: 0
    };

    this.increase = this.increase.bind(this);
  }

  increase(e) {
    this.setState({
      count: this.state.count + 1
    });
  }

  render() {
    var backgroundStyle = {
      padding: 50,
      backgroundColor: "#FFC53A",
      width: 250,
      height: 100,
      borderRadius: 10,
      textAlign: "center"
    };

    var buttonStyle = {
      fontSize: "1em",
      width: 30,
```

```
      height: 30,
      fontFamily: "sans-serif",
      color: "#333",
      fontWeight: "bold",
      lineHeight: "3px"
    };

    return (
      <div style={backgroundStyle}>
        <Counter display={this.state.count} />
        <button onClick={this.increase} style={buttonStyle}>+</button>
      </div>
    );
  }
}
```

All we're doing with these lines is making sure that each call to the `increase` function increments the value of our `this.state.count` property by 1. Because we're dealing with events,
our `increase` function (as the designated event handler) will get access to any event arguments. We've set these arguments to be accessed by `e`, and you can see that by looking at our
`increase` function's signature (that is, what its declaration looks like). We'll talk about the
various events and their properties in a little bit when we take a detailed look at Events. Lastly,
in the constructor, we bind the value of this to the `increase` function.

Now, go ahead and preview what you have in your browser. Once everything has loaded, click
the plus button to see our newly added code in action. The counter value should increase with
each click. Isn't that pretty awesome?

Event Properties

As you know, events pass what are known as event arguments to our event handlers. These
event arguments contain a bunch of properties that are specific to the type of event you're
dealing with. In the regular DOM world, each event has its own type. For example, if you're
dealing with a mouse event, your event and its event arguments object are of type `MouseEvent`.
This `MouseEvent` object allows you to access mouse-specific information, such as which button
was pressed or the screen position of the mouse click. Event arguments for a keyboard-related
event are of type `KeyboardEvent`. Your `KeyboardEvent` object contains properties that (among
many other things) allow you to figure out which key was actually pressed. I could go on
forever for every other event type, but you get the point. Each event type contains its own set
of properties that you can access via the event handler for that event.

Why am I boring you with things you already know? Well....

Meet Synthetic Events

In React, when you specify an event in JSX as we did with `onClick`, you're not directly dealing with regular DOM events. Instead, you're dealing with a React-specific event type known as a `SyntheticEvent`. Your event handlers don't get native event arguments of type `MouseEvent`, `KeyboardEvent`, and so on. They always get event arguments of type `SyntheticEvent` that wrap your browser's native event instead. What's the fallout of this in our code? Surprisingly not a whole lot.

Each `SyntheticEvent` contains the following properties:

```
boolean bubbles
boolean cancelable
DOMEventTarget currentTarget
boolean defaultPrevented
number eventPhase
boolean isTrusted
DOMEvent nativeEvent
void preventDefault()
boolean isDefaultPrevented()
void stopPropagation()
boolean isPropagationStopped()
DOMEventTarget target
number timeStamp
string type
```

These properties should seem pretty straightforward...and generic! The nongeneric stuff depends on what type of native event our `SyntheticEvent` is wrapping. This means that a `SyntheticEvent` that wraps a `MouseEvent` will have access to mouse-specific properties such as the following:

```
boolean altKey
number button
number buttons
number clientX
number clientY
boolean ctrlKey
boolean getModifierState(key)
boolean metaKey
number pageX
number pageY
DOMEventTarget relatedTarget
number screenX
number screenY
boolean shiftKey
```

Similarly, a `SyntheticEvent` that wraps a `KeyboardEvent` will have access to these additional keyboard-related properties:

```
boolean altKey
number charCode
boolean ctrlKey
boolean getModifierState(key)
string key
number keyCode
string locale
number location
boolean metaKey
boolean repeat
boolean shiftKey
number which
```

In the end, all of this means that you still get the same functionality in the `SyntheticEvent` world that you had in the vanilla DOM world.

Now, here's something I learned the hard way: *Don't refer to traditional DOM event documentation when using `SyntheticEvents` and their properties.* Because the `SyntheticEvent` wraps your native DOM event, events and their properties might not map one-to-one. Some DOM events don't even exist in React. To avoid running into any issues, if you want to know the name of a `SyntheticEvent` or any of its properties, *refer to the React Event System document (https://facebook.github.io/react/docs/events.html)* instead.

Doing Stuff with Event Properties

By now, you've seen more about the DOM and SyntheticEvents than you'd probably like. To wash away the taste of all that text, let's write some code and put your newfound knowledge to good use. Right now, our counter example increments by 1 each time you click the plus button. We want to *increment our counter by 10 when the Shift key on the keyboard is pressed* while clicking the plus button with our mouse.

We can do that by using the `shiftKey` property that exists on the `SyntheticEvent` when using the mouse:

```
boolean altKey
number button
number buttons
number clientX
number clientY
boolean ctrlKey
boolean getModifierState(key)
boolean metaKey
number pageX
number pageY
```

```
DOMEventTarget relatedTarget
number screenX
number screenY
boolean shiftKey
```

The way this property works is simple. If the Shift key is pressed when this mouse event fires, then the shiftKey property value is true. Otherwise, the shiftKey property value is false. To increment our counter by 10 when the Shift key is pressed, go back to our increase function and make the following highlighted changes:

```
increase(e) {
  var currentCount = this.state.count;

  if (e.shiftKey) {
    currentCount += 10;
  } else {
    currentCount += 1;
  }

  this.setState({
    count: currentCount
  });
}
```

When you've made the changes, preview the example in the browser. Each time you click the plus button, your counter will increment by 1 just like always. If you click on the plus button with your Shift key pressed, notice that the counter increments by 10 instead.

All of this works because we change our incrementing behavior depending on whether the Shift key is pressed. That's primarily handled by the following lines:

```
if (e.shiftKey) {
  currentCount += 10;
} else {
  currentCount += 1;
}
```

If the shiftKey property on our SyntheticEvent event argument is true, we increment our counter by 10. If the shiftKey value is false, we just increment by 1.

More Eventing Shenanigans

We're not done yet! Up to this point, we've looked at how to work with events in React in a very simplistic way. In the real world, things rarely will be as direct as what you've seen. Your real apps will be more complex, and because React insists on doing things differently, you'll need to learn (or relearn) some new event-related tricks and techniques to make your apps work. That's where this section comes in. We're going to look at some common situations you'll run into and how to deal with them.

You Can't Directly Listen to Events on Components

Let's say your component is nothing more than a button or another type of UI element that users will be interacting with. You can't get away with doing something like what we see in the following highlighted line:

```
class CounterParent extends React.Component {
  constructor(props) {
    super(props);

    this.state = {
      count: 0
    };

    this.increase = this.increase.bind(this);
  }

  increase(e) {
    this.setState({
      count: this.state.count + 1
    });
  }

  render() {
    return (
      <div>
        <Counter display={this.state.count} />
        <PlusButton onClick={this.increase} />
      </div>
    );
  }
}
```

On the surface, this line of JSX looks totally valid. When somebody clicks our `PlusButton` component, the `increase` function gets called. In case you're curious, this is what our `PlusButton` component looks like:

```
class PlusButton extends React.Component {
  render() {
    return (
      <button>
        +
      </button>
    );
  }
}
```

Our `PlusButton` component doesn't do anything crazy; it only returns a single HTML element.

No matter how you slice and dice this, none of it matters. It doesn't matter how simple or obvious the HTML we're returning via a component looks. *You simply can't listen for events on them directly.* This is because components are wrappers for DOM elements. What does it even mean to listen for an event on a component? When your component gets unwrapped into DOM elements, does the outer HTML element act as the thing you're listening for the event on? Is it some other element? How do you distinguish between listening for an event and declaring a prop you're listening for?

There's no clear answer to any of those questions. It's too harsh to say that the solution is to simply not listen to events on components, either. Fortunately, there's a workaround: We can treat the event handler as a prop and pass it on to the component. Inside the component, we can then assign the event to a DOM element and set the event handler to the value of the prop we just passed in. I realize that probably makes no sense, so let's walk through an example.

Take a look at the following highlighted line:

```
class CounterParent extends React.Component {
  .
  .
  .
  render() {
    return (
      <div>
        <Counter display={this.state.count} />
        <PlusButton clickHandler={this.increase} />
      </div>
    );
  }
}
```

In this example, we create a property called `clickHandler` whose value is the `increase` event handler. Inside our `PlusButton` component, we can then do something like this:

```
class PlusButton extends React.Component {
  render() {
    return (
      <button onClick={this.props.clickHandler}>
        +
      </button>
    );
  }
}
```

On our button element, we specify the `onClick` event and set its value to the `clickHandler` prop. At runtime, this prop gets evaluated as our `increase` function, and clicking the plus button ensures that the `increase` function gets called. This solves our problem while still allowing our component to participate in all this eventing goodness.

Listening to Regular DOM Events

If you thought the previous section was a doozy, wait until you see what we have here. Not all DOM events have `SyntheticEvent` equivalents. It might seem like you can just add the `on` prefix and capitalize the event you're listening for when specifying it inline in your JSX:

```
class Something extends React.Component {
  .
  .
  .
  handleMyEvent(e) {
    // do something
  }

  render() {
    return (
      <div onSomeEvent={this.handleMyEvent}>Hello!</div>
    );
  }
}
```

It doesn't work that way! For events that React doesn't officially recognize, you have to follow the traditional approach that uses `addEventListener` with a few extra hoops to jump through.

Take a look at the following section of code:

```
class Something extends React.Component {
  .
  .
  .
  handleMyEvent(e) {
    // do something
  }

  componentDidMount() {
    window.addEventListener("someEvent", this.handleMyEvent);
  }

  componentWillUnmount() {
    window.removeEventListener("someEvent", this.handleMyEvent);
  }

  render() {
    return (
      <div>Hello!</div>
    );
  }
}
```

We have our `Something` component that listens for an event called `someEvent`. We start listening for this event under the `componentDidMount` method, which is automatically called when our component gets rendered. We listen for our event by using `addEventListener` and specifying both the event and the event handler to call.

That should be pretty straightforward. The only other point you need to keep in mind is that you need to remove the event listener when the component is about to be destroyed. To do that, you can use the opposite of the `componentDidMount` method, the `componentWillUnmount` method. Put your `removeEventListener` call inside that method to ensure that no trace of our event listening exists after our component goes away.

The Meaning of `this` Inside the Event Handler

When dealing with events in React, the value of `this` inside your event handler is different than what you normally see in the non-React DOM world. In the non-React world, the value of `this` inside an event handler refers to the element that fired the event:

```
function doSomething(e) {
  console.log(this); // button element
}

var foo = document.querySelector("button");
foo.addEventListener("click", doSomething, false);
```

In the React world, the value of `this` does not refer to the element that fired the event. The value is the very unhelpful (yet correct) `undefined`. That's why we need to explicitly specify what this binds to using the `bind` method, as you've seen a few times:

```
class CounterParent extends React.Component {
  constructor(props) {
    super(props);

    this.state = {
      count: 0
    };

    this.increase = this.increase.bind(this);
  }

  increase(e) {
    console.log(this);

    this.setState({
      count: this.state.count + 1
    });
  }
```

```
render() {
  return (
    <div>
      <Counter display={this.state.count} />
      <button onClick={this.increase}>+</button>
    </div>
  );
  }
}
```

In this example, the value of this inside the increase event handler refers to the
CounterParent component. It doesn't refer to the element that triggered the event. You can
attribute this behavior to us binding the value of this to our component from inside our
constructor.

React...Why? Why?

Before we call it a day, let's use this time to talk about why React decided to deviate from how
we've worked with events in the past. There are two reasons:

1. Browser compatibility

2. Improved performance

Let's elaborate on these reasons a bit.

Browser Compatibility

Event handling is one of those things that works consistently in modern browsers, but once
you go back to older browser versions, things get really bad really quickly. By wrapping all the
native events as an object of type SyntheticEvent, React frees you from dealing with event-
handling quirks.

Improved Performance

In complex UIs, the more event handlers you have, the more memory your app takes up.
Manually dealing with that isn't difficult, but it is a bit tedious as you try to group events under
a common parent. Sometimes that just isn't possible. Sometimes the hassle doesn't outweigh
the benefits. What React does is pretty clever.

React never directly attaches event handlers to the DOM elements. *It uses one event handler at
the root of your document* that is responsible for listening to all events and calling the appropriate
event handler as necessary (see Figure 10.3).

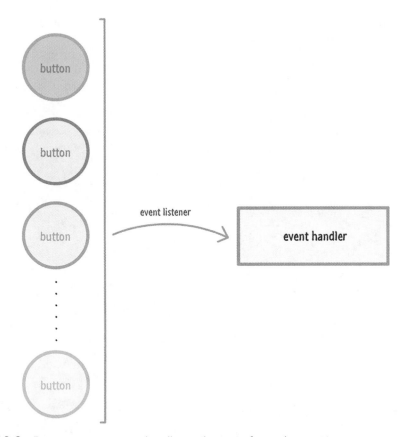

Figure 10.3   React uses one event handler at the root of your document.

This frees you from having to deal with optimizing your event handler–related code yourself. If you've manually had to do that in the past, you can relax, knowing that React takes care of that tedious task for you. If you've never had to optimize event handler–related code yourself, consider yourself lucky.

Conclusion

You'll spend a good amount of time dealing with events, and this chapter threw a lot of things at you. We started by exploring the basics of how to listen to events and specify the event handler. Toward the end, we got fully invested and looked at eventing corner cases that you'll bump into if you aren't careful enough. You don't want to bump into corners. That's never fun.

Note: If you run into any issues, ask!

If you have any questions or your code isn't running like you expect, don't hesitate to ask! Post on the forums at https://forum.kirupa.com and get help from some of the friendliest and most knowledgeable people the Internet has ever brought together!

11

The Component Lifecycle

In the beginning, we took a very simple view of components and what they do. As you learned more about React and did cooler and more involved things, you came to see that components aren't all that simple. They help us deal with properties, state, and events, and often are responsible for the well-being of other components as well. Keeping track of everything components do sometimes can be tough.

To help with this, React provides us with lifecycle methods. Unsurprisingly, **lifecycle methods** are special methods that automatically get called as our component goes about its business. They notify us of important milestones in a component's life, and we can use these notifications to simply pay attention or change what our component is about to do.

In this chapter, we look at these lifecycle methods and talk about what we can do with them.

> ### Note: Changes Are a Foot Here!
>
> There are proposed changes in this area that will change how lifecycle methods behave. What you see printed here is based on the latest guidance, but note that this information may change. Visit this link to be kept up-to-date: http://bit.ly/lifecycleChanges.

Meet the Lifecycle Methods

Lifecycle methods aren't very complicated. You can think of them as glorified event handlers that get called at various points in a component's life. As with event handlers, you can write some code to do things at those various points. Before we go further, it's time for you to quickly meet our lifecycle methods:

- componentWillMount
- componentDidMount
- componentWillUnmount
- componentWillUpdate
- componentDidUpdate
- shouldComponentUpdate
- componentWillReceiveProps
- componentDidCatch

We aren't quite done yet. We're going to throw one other method into the mix even though it isn't strictly a lifecycle method: the infamous `render` method.

Some of these names probably sound familiar to you, and some you're probably seeing for the first time. Don't worry. By the end of all this, you'll be on a first-name basis with all of them! We're going to look at these lifecycle methods from various angles, starting with some code.

See the Lifecycle Methods in Action

Learning about these lifecycle methods is about as exciting as memorizing names for foreign places you have no plans to visit. To make all of this more bearable, let's play with them in a simple example before we get all academic and read about them.

To play with this example, go to the following URL: https://www.kirupa.com/react/ lifecycle_example.htm. When this page loads, you'll see a variation of the counter example you saw earlier (see Figure 11.1).

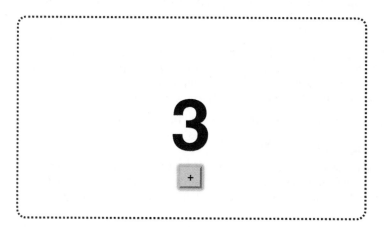

Figure 11.1   A variation on the counter example.

Don't click the button or anything just yet. (If you've already clicked the button, just refresh the page to start the example from the beginning.) I'm saying this for a reason, and it isn't because my OCD is acting up. You want to see this page as it is before you interact with it.

Now bring up your browser's developer tools and take a look at the Console tab. In Chrome, you'll see something that looks like Figure 11.2.

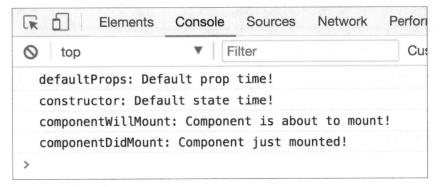

Figure 11.2   The Console view in Chrome.

Notice what you see printed. You see some messages, and these messages start with the name of what looks like a lifecycle method. If you click the plus button now, notice that your Console shows more lifecycle methods getting called (see Figure 11.3).

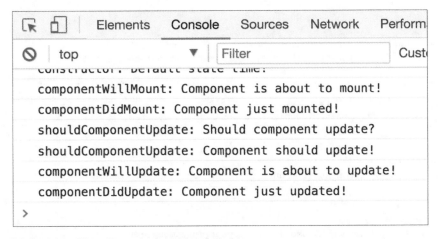

Figure 11.3   More lifecycle methods getting called.

Play with this example for a bit. You can see that it allows you to place all of these lifecycle methods in the context of a component that you've already seen. As you keep clicking the plus button, more lifecycle method entries show up. Eventually, when your counter approaches a value of 5, your example disappears and the following entry shows up in your console: `componentWillUnmount: Component is about to be removed from the DOM!` At this point, you've reached the end of this example. Of course, to start over, you can just refresh the page.

Now that you've seen the example, let's take a quick look at the component that's responsible for all of this (full source: https://github.com/kirupa/kirupa/blob/master/reactjs/lifecycle.htm):

```
class CounterParent extends React.Component {
  constructor(props) {
    super(props);

    console.log("constructor: Default state time!");

    this.state = {
      count: 0
    };

    this.increase = this.increase.bind(this);
  }

  increase() {
    this.setState({
      count: this.state.count + 1
    });
  }

  componentWillUpdate(newProps, newState) {
    console.log("componentWillUpdate: Component is about to update!");
  }

  componentDidUpdate(currentProps, currentState) {
    console.log("componentDidUpdate: Component just updated!");
  }

  componentWillMount() {
    console.log("componentWillMount: Component is about to mount!");
  }

  componentDidMount() {
    console.log("componentDidMount: Component just mounted!");
  }

  componentWillUnmount() {
    console.log("componentWillUnmount: Component is about to be removed from the DOM!");
  }

  shouldComponentUpdate(newProps, newState) {
    console.log("shouldComponentUpdate: Should component update?");
```

```
    if (newState.count < 5) {
      console.log("shouldComponentUpdate: Component should update!");
      return true;
    } else {
      ReactDOM.unmountComponentAtNode(destination);
      console.log("shouldComponentUpdate: Component should not update!");
      return false;
    }
  }

  componentWillReceiveProps(newProps) {
    console.log("componentWillReceiveProps: Component will get new props!");
  }

  render() {
    var backgroundStyle = {
      padding: 50,
      border: "#333 2px dotted",
      width: 250,
      height: 100,
      borderRadius: 10,
      textAlign: "center"
    };

    return (
      <div style={backgroundStyle}>
        <Counter display={this.state.count} />
        <button onClick={this.increase}>
          +
        </button>
      </div>
    );
  }
}

console.log("defaultProps: Default prop time!");
CounterParent.defaultProps = {

};
```

Take a few moments to understand what all this code does. It seems lengthy, but the bulk of it is just each lifecycle method listed with a `console.log` statement defined. After you've gone through this code, play with the example one more time. Trust me. *The more time you spend in the example to figure out what's going on, the more fun you'll have.* The following sections will be dreadfully boring when we look at each lifecycle method across the rendering, updating, and unmounting phases. Don't say I didn't warn you.

The Initial Rendering Phase

When your component is about to start its life and make its way to the DOM, the following lifecycle methods get called (see Figure 11.4).

Initial Render

begin | Default Props

Get State

componentWillMount

render

end | componentDidMount

Figure 11.4   The lifecycle methods called initially.

What you saw in your console when the example was loaded was a less colorful version of what you saw here. Now let's go a bit further and see more about what each lifecycle methods does.

Getting the Default Props

This property on the component allows you to specify the default value of `this.props`. If we wanted to set a name property on our `CounterParent` component, it could look as follows:

```
CounterParent.defaultProps = {
  name: "Iron Man"
};
```

This gets run before your component is even created or any props from parent components are passed in.

Getting the Default State

This step happens inside your component's constructor. You get the chance to specify the default value of `this.state` as part of your component's creation:

```
constructor(props) {
  super(props);

  console.log("constructor: Default state time!");

  this.state = {
    count: 0
  };

  this.increase = this.increase.bind(this);
}
```

Notice that we're defining our `state` object and initializing it with a `count` property whose value is `0`.

componentWillMount

This is the last method that gets called before your component gets rendered to the DOM. There's an important point to note here: If you call `setState` inside this method, your component will not re-render.

render

This one should be very familiar to you by now. Every component must have this method defined, and it is responsible for returning some JSX. If you don't want to render anything, simply return `null` or `false`.

componentDidMount

This method gets called immediately after your component renders and gets placed on the DOM. At this point, you can safely perform any DOM querying operations without worrying about whether your component has made it. If you have any code that depends on your component being ready, you can specify all of that code here as well.

With the exception of the `render` method, all of these lifecycle methods *can fire only once*. That's quite different from the methods you see next.

The Updating Phase

After your components get added to the DOM, they can potentially update and re-render when a prop or state change occurs. During this time, a different collection of lifecycle methods gets called. Yawn. Sorry...

Dealing with State Changes

First, let's look at a state change. As we mentioned earlier, when a state change occurs, your component calls its `render` method again. Any components that rely on the output of this component also get their `render` methods called. This is done to ensure that the component is always displaying the latest version of itself. All of that is true, but it's only a partial representation of what happens.

When a state change happens, all the lifecycle methods in Figure 11.5 get called.

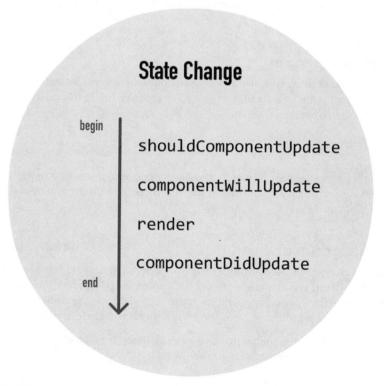

Figure 11.5　Lifecycle methods called when a state change happens.

Check out what these lifecycle methods do:

shouldComponentUpdate

Sometimes you don't want your component to update when a state change occurs. This method allows you to control this updating behavior. If you use this method and return a `true` value, the component will update. If this method returns a `false` value, this component will skip updating.

That probably sounds a bit confusing, so take a look at a simple snippet:

```
shouldComponentUpdate(newProps, newState) {
  console.log("shouldComponentUpdate: Should component update?");

  if (newState.count < 5) {
    console.log("shouldComponentUpdate: Component should update!");
    return true;
  } else {
    ReactDOM.unmountComponentAtNode(destination);
    console.log("shouldComponentUpdate: Component should not update!");
    return false;
  }
}
```

This method gets called with two arguments, which we named `newProps` and `newState`. In this snippet of code, we check whether the new value of our `id state` property is less than or equal to 2. If the value is less than or equal to 2, we return `true` to indicate that this component should update. If the value is not less than or equal to 2, we return `false` to indicate that this component should not update.

componentWillUpdate

This method gets called just before your component is about to update. Nothing too exciting happens here. One point to note is that you can't change your state by calling `this.setState` from this method.

render

If you didn't override the update via `shouldComponentUpdate`, the code inside `render` gets called again to ensure that your component displays itself properly.

componentDidUpdate

This method gets called after your component updates and the `render` method has been called. If you need to execute any code after the update takes place, this is the place to stash it.

Dealing with Prop Changes

The other time your component updates is when its prop value changes after it has been rendered into the DOM. In this scenario, the lifecycle methods in Figure 11.6 get called.

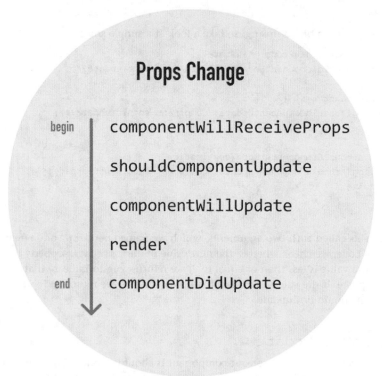

Props Change

begin   componentWillReceiveProps

shouldComponentUpdate

componentWillUpdate

render

end   componentDidUpdate

Figure 11.6   Lifecycle methods when the component's prop value changes.

The only new method here is componentWillReceiveProps. This method receives one argument, and this argument contains the new prop value that is about to be assigned to it.

You saw the rest of the lifecycle methods when looking at state changes, so let's not revisit them. Their behavior is identical when dealing with a prop change.

The Unmounting Phase

The last phase to look at is when your component is about to be destroyed and removed from the DOM (see Figure 11.7).

Only one lifecycle method is active here, and that is componentWillUnmount. You perform cleanup-related tasks here, such as removing event listeners and stopping timers. After this method gets called, your component is removed from the DOM and you can say goodbye to it.

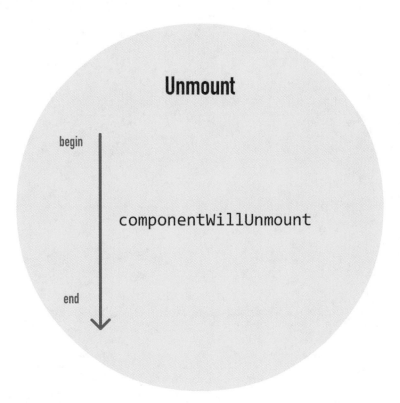

Figure 11.7   Only one lifecycle method is active when your component is about to be destroyed and removed from the DOM.

Conclusion

Components are fascinating little things. On the surface, they seem like they don't have much going on. As in a good documentary about the oceans, when we look a little deeper and closer, it's almost like seeing a whole other world. As it turns out, React is constantly watching and notifying your component every time something interesting happens. All of this is done via the (extremely boring) lifecycle methods that we spent this entire tutorial looking at. Now, I want to reassure you that knowing what each lifecycle method does and when it gets called will come in handy one day. All that you've learned isn't just trivial knowledge, although your friends will be impressed if you can describe every lifecycle method from memory. Go ahead and try it the next time you see them.

Note: If you run into any issues, ask!

If you have any questions or your code isn't running like you expect, don't hesitate to ask! Post on the forums at https://forum.kirupa.com and get help from some of the friendliest and most knowledgeable people the Internet has ever brought together!

12

Accessing DOM Elements in React

Sometimes you want to access properties and methods on an HTML element directly. In our React-colored world, where JSX represents everything that is good and pure about markup, why would you ever want to deal directly with the horribleness that is HTML? As you will find out (if you haven't already), in many cases, dealing with HTML elements through the JavaScript DOM API directly is easier than fiddling with "the React way" of doing things. To highlight one such situation, take a look at the Colorizer example in Figure 12.1.

Figure 12.1   Colorizer example.

If you have access to a browser, you can view it live at the following location:
https://www.kirupa.com/react/examples/colorizer.htm.

The **Colorizer** colorizes the (currently) white square with whatever color you provide it. To see
it in action, enter a color value inside the text field and click/tap the Go button. (If you don't
have any idea of what color to enter, yellow is a good one.) After you provide a color and
submit it, the white square turns whatever color value you provided (see Figure 12.2).

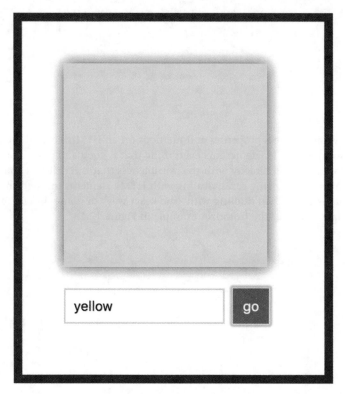

Figure 12.2   The white square turns yellow.

The fact that the square changes color for any valid color value you submit is pretty awesome,
but that isn't what you should focus on. Instead, pay attention to the text field and the button
after you submit a value. Notice that the button gets focus, and the color value you just
submitted is still displayed inside the form. If you want to enter another color value, you need
to explicitly return focus to the text field and clear out whatever current value is present. Eww!
That seems unnecessary, and we can do better than that from a usability point of view.

Wouldn't it be great if we could both clear the existing color value and return focus to the text
field immediately after submitting a color? That would mean that if we submitted a color value
of purple, afterward we would see something that looks like Figure 12.3.

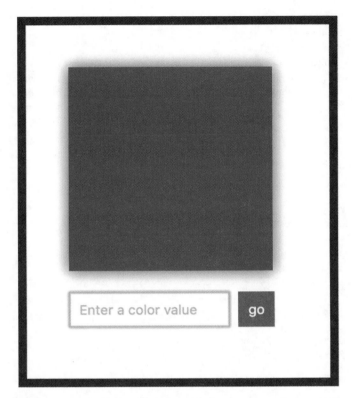

Figure 12.3   We get purple and the text field is ready for the next color.

The entered value of purple is cleared and the focus is returned to the text field. This allows us to enter additional color values and submit them easily without having to keep jumping back and forth between the text field and the button. Isn't that much nicer?

Getting this behavior right using JSX and traditional React techniques is hard. We aren't even going to bother explaining how to go about it. On the other hand, getting this behavior right by dealing with the JavaScript DOM API on various HTML elements directly is pretty easy. Guess what we're going to do? In the following sections, we're going to use something known as refs, which React provides to help us access the DOM API on HTML elements. We'll also look at portals, which allow us to render content to any HTML element on the page.

The Colorizer Example

To explain refs and portals, we'll be modifying the Colorizer example you saw earlier. The code for it looks as follows:

```
<!DOCTYPE html>
<html>
```

```
<head>
  <meta charset="utf-8">
  <title>The Colorizer!</title>
  <script src="https://unpkg.com/react@16/umd/react.development.js"></script>
  <script src="https://unpkg.com/react-dom@16/umd/react-dom.development.js"></script>
  <script src="https://unpkg.com/babel-standalone@6.15.0/babel.min.js"></script>

  <style>
    #container {
      padding: 50px;
      background-color: #FFF;
    }

    .colorSquare {
      box-shadow: 0px 0px 25px 0px #333;
      width: 242px;
      height: 242px;
      margin-bottom: 15px;
    }

    .colorArea input {
      padding: 10px;
      font-size: 16px;
      border: 2px solid #CCC;
    }

    .colorArea button {
      padding: 10px;
      font-size: 16px;
      margin: 10px;
      background-color: #666;
      color: #FFF;
      border: 2px solid #666;
    }

    .colorArea button:hover {
      background-color: #111;
      border-color: #111;
      cursor: pointer;
    }
  </style>
</head>

<body>
  <div id="container"></div>
  <script type="text/babel">
```

```
class Colorizer extends React.Component {
  constructor(props) {
    super(props);

    this.state = {
      color: "",
      bgColor: "white"
    };

    this.colorValue = this.colorValue.bind(this);
    this.setNewColor = this.setNewColor.bind(this);
  }

  colorValue(e) {
    this.setState({
      color: e.target.value
    });
  }

  setNewColor(e) {
    this.setState({
      bgColor: this.state.color
    });

    e.preventDefault();
  }

  render() {
    var squareStyle = {
      backgroundColor: this.state.bgColor
    };

    return (
      <div className="colorArea">
        <div style={squareStyle} className="colorSquare"></div>

        <form onSubmit={this.setNewColor}>
          <input onChange={this.colorValue}
            placeholder="Enter a color value"></input>
          <button type="submit">go</button>
        </form>
      </div>
    );
  }
}
```

```
    ReactDOM.render(
      <div>
        <Colorizer />
      </div>,
      document.querySelector("#container")
    );
  </script>
</body>

</html>
```

Take a few moments to look through the code and see how it maps to our example. You shouldn't find anything surprising here. Once you've gotten a good understanding of this code, it's time to learn about refs.

Meet Refs

As you know very well by now, inside our various render methods we've been writing HTML-like `things` known as JSX. Our JSX is simply a description of what the DOM should look like. It doesn't represent actual HTML, despite looking a whole lot like it. To provide a bridge between JSX and the final HTML elements in the DOM, React provides us with something funnily named as refs (short for *references*).

The way refs works is a little odd. The easiest way to make sense of it is to just use it. Take a look at just the `render` method from our Colorizer example:

```
render() {
  var squareStyle = {
    backgroundColor: this.state.bgColor
  };

  return (
    <div className="colorArea">
      <div style={squareStyle} className="colorSquare"></div>

      <form onSubmit={this.setNewColor}>
        <input onChange={this.colorValue}
               placeholder="Enter a color value"></input>
        <button type="submit">go</button>
      </form>
    </div>
  );
}
```

Inside this `render` method, we are returning a big chunk of JSX representing (among other things) the `input` element where we enter our color value. We want to access the input element's DOM representation so that we can call some APIs on it using JavaScript.

The way we do that using refs is by setting the `ref` attribute on the element whose HTML we want to reference:

```
render() {
  var squareStyle = {
    backgroundColor: this.state.bgColor
  };

  return (
    <div className="colorArea">
      <div style={squareStyle} className="colorSquare"></div>  `

      <form onSubmit={this.setNewColor}>
        <input onChange={this.colorValue}
               ref={}
               placeholder="Enter a color value"></input>
        <button type="submit">go</button>
      </form>
    </div>
  );
}
```

Because we're interested in the `input` element, our `ref` attribute is attached to it. Right now, our `ref` attribute is empty. What you typically set as the `ref` attribute's value is a JavaScript callback function. This function gets called automatically when the component housing this `render` method gets mounted. If we set our `ref` attribute's value to a simple JavaScript function that stores a reference to the referenced DOM element, it would look something like the following highlighted lines:

```
render() {
  var squareStyle = {
    backgroundColor: this.state.bgColor
  };

  var self = this;

  return (
    <div className="colorArea">
      <div style={squareStyle} className="colorSquare"></div>

      <form onSubmit={this.setNewColor}>
        <input onChange={this.colorValue}
               ref={
                 function(el) {
```

```
                    self._input = el;
                }
            }
            placeholder="Enter a color value"></input>
        <button type="submit">go</button>
      </form>
    </div>
  );
}
```

The end result of this code running once our component mounts is simple: We can access
the HTML representing our input element from anywhere inside our component by using
self._input. Take a few moments to see how the highlighted lines of code help do
that. When you're done, we'll walk through this code together.

First, our callback function looks as follows:

```
function(el) {
 self._input = el;
}
```

This anonymous function gets called when our component mounts, and a reference to the
final HTML DOM element is passed in as an argument. We capture this argument using the el
identifier, but you can use any name for this argument that you want. The body of this callback
function simply sets a custom property called _input to the value of our DOM element. To
ensure that we create this property on our component, we use the self variable to create a
closure—the this in question refers to our component instead of the callback function itself.
Phew!

Let's focus on what we can do now that we have access to our input element. Our goal is to
clear the contents of our input element and give focus to it once the form gets submitted. The
code for doing that will live in our setNewColor method, so add the following highlighted
lines:

```
setNewColor(e) {
  this.setState({
    bgColor: this.state.color
  });

  this._input.focus();
  this._input.value = "";

  e.preventDefault();
}
```

Calling this._input.value = "" clears the color we entered. We set focus back to our input
element by calling this._input.focus(). All our ref-related work was to simply enable these
two lines; we needed some way to have this._input point to the HTML element representing
our input element that we defined in JSX. Then we can just call the value property and focus
method that the DOM API exposes on this element.

Simplifying Further with ES6 Arrow Functions

Learning React is hard enough, so I've tried to avoid forcing you to use ES6 techniques by default. When it comes to working with the `ref` attribute, using arrow functions to deal with the callback function simplifies matters a bit. This is one of those cases for which I recommend you use an ES6 technique.

As you saw a few moments ago, to assign a property on our component to the referenced HTML element, we did something like this:

```
<input
    ref={
        function(el) {
          self._input = el;
        }
      }>
</input>
```

To deal with context shenanigans, we created a `self` variable initialized to `this`, to ensure that we created the `_input` property on our component. That seems unnecessarily messy.

Using arrow functions, we can simplify all of this down to just the following:

```
<input
    ref={
        (el) => this._input = el
      }>
</input>
```

The end result is identical to what we spent all this time looking at. Because of how arrow functions deal with context, you can use this inside the function body and reference the component without doing any extra work. No need for an outer `self` variable equivalent!

Using Portals

You need to be aware of one more DOM-related trick. So far, we've been dealing with HTML only in the context of what our JSX generates, either from a single component or combined through many components. This means we're limited by the DOM hierarchy our parent components impose on us. Having arbitrary access to any DOM element anywhere on the page doesn't seem possible. Or is it? As it turns out, you can choose to render your JSX to any DOM element anywhere on the page; you aren't limited to just sending your JSX to a parent component. The magic behind this wizardry is a feature known as **portals**.

The way we use a portal is very similar to what we do with our `ReactDOM.render` method. We specify the JSX we want to render, and we specify the DOM element we want to render to.

To see all of this in action, go back to our example and add the following `h1` element as a sibling just above where we have our `container` `div` element defined:

```
<body>

  <h1 id="colorHeading">Colorizer</h1>

  <div id="container"></div>
    .
    .
    .
```

Next, add the following style rule inside the `style` tag to make our `h1` element look nicer:

```
#colorHeading {
  padding: 0;
  margin: 50px;
  margin-bottom: -20px;
  font-family: sans-serif;
}
```

With this style rule added, let's first preview our app to make sure that the HTML and CSS we added look as expected (Figure 12.4):

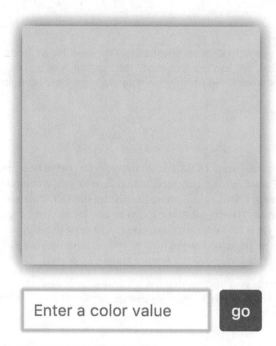

Figure 12.4   What our example looks like currently!

Here's what we want to do. We want to change the value of our h1 element to display the name of the color we are currently previewing. The point to emphasize is that our h1 element is a sibling of the container div element where our app is set to render into.

To accomplish what we're trying to do, go back to our Colorizer component's render method and add the following highlighted line to the return statement:

```
return (
  <div className="colorArea">
    <div style={squareStyle} className="colorSquare"></div>

    <form onSubmit={this.setNewColor}>
      <input onChange={this.colorValue}
             ref={
               function(el) {
                 self._input = el;
               }
             }
             placeholder="Enter a color value"></input>
      <button type="submit">go</button>
    </form>
    <ColorLabel color={this.state.bgColor}/>
  </div>
);
```

Here we're instantiating a component called ColorLabel and declaring a prop called color with its value set to our bgColor state property. We haven't created this component yet, so to fix that, add the following lines just above where we have our ReactDOM.render call:

```
var heading = document.querySelector("#colorHeading");

class ColorLabel extends React.Component {
  render() {
    return ReactDOM.createPortal(
      ": " + this.props.color,
      heading
    );
  }
}
```

We are referencing our h1 element with the heading variable. That's old stuff. For the new stuff, take a look at our ColorLabel component's render method. More specifically, notice what our return statement looks like. We are returning the result of calling ReactDOM.createPortal():

```
class ColorLabel extends React.Component {
  render() {
    return ReactDOM.createPortal(
```

```
      ": " + this.props.color,
      heading
    );
  }
}
```

The `ReactDOM.createPortal()` method takes two arguments: the JSX to print and the DOM element to print that JSX to. The JSX we are printing is just some formatting characters and the color value we passed in as a prop:

```
class ColorLabel extends React.Component {
  render() {
    return ReactDOM.createPortal(
      ": " + this.props.color,
      heading
    );
  }
}
```

The DOM element we are printing all of this to is our `h1` element referenced by the `heading` variable:

```
class ColorLabel extends React.Component {
  render() {
    return ReactDOM.createPortal(
      ": " + this.props.color,
      heading
    );
  }
}
```

When you preview your app and change the color, notice what happens. The color we specified in our input element shows up in the heading (Figure 12.5):

Colorizer: yellow

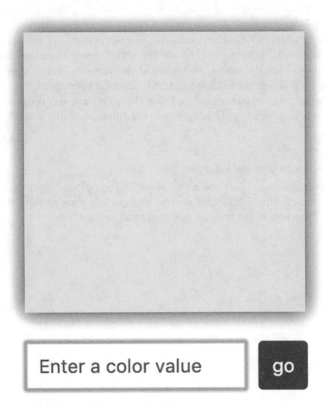

Enter a color value   go

Figure 12.5   Our header now contains our color element.

The important part to re-emphasize is that our h1 element is outside the scope of our main React app, which prints to our container div element. By relying on portals, we have direct access to any element in our page's DOM and can render content into it, bypassing the traditional parent/child hierarchy we've been living under so far.

Conclusion

Most of the time, everything you want to do will be within arm's reach of the JSX you're writing. Sometimes, though, you need to break free from the box React puts you in. Even though everything we're creating is rendering to a HTML document, our React app is like a self-sufficient tropical island within the document; you never quite see the actual HTML that lies just beneath the sands. To help you both see the HTML inside the island and make contact with things that live outside the island, we looked at two features, **refs** and **portals**. Refs allow you to cut through and access the underlying HTML element behind the JSX. Portals allow you to render your content to any element in the DOM that you have access to. Between these two solutions, you should be able to easily address any need that you have to deal with regards to the DOM directly.

> **Note: If you run into any issues, ask!**
>
> If you have any questions or your code isn't running like you expect, don't hesitate to ask! Post on the forums at https://forum.kirupa.com and get help from some of the friendliest and most knowledgeable people the Internet has ever brought together!

13

Setting Up Your React Dev Environment Easily

The last major new topic we're going to look at is less about React and more about setting up your development environment to build a React app. Until now, we've been building our React apps by including a few script files:

```
<script src="https://unpkg.com/react@16/umd/react.development.js"></script>
<script src="https://unpkg.com/react-dom@16/umd/react-dom.development.js"></script>
<script src="https://unpkg.com/babel-standalone@6.15.0/babel.min.js"></script>
```

These script files not only loaded the React libraries, but they also loaded Babel to help our browser do what needs to be done when encountering bizarre things like JSX (Figure 13.1):

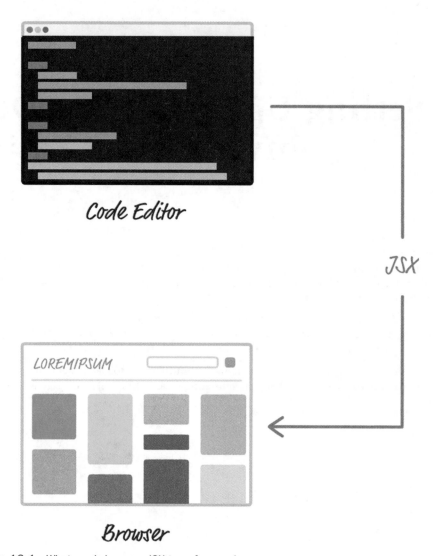

Figure 13.1   What our in-browser JSX transformer does.

To review what we mentioned earlier when talking about this approach, the downside is performance. As your browser handles all of the page loading things it normally does, it is also responsible for turning your JSX into actual JavaScript. That conversion is a time-consuming process that is fine during development but not fine if every user of your app has to pay that performance penalty.

The solution is to set up your development environment so that your JSX-to-JS conversion is handled as part of getting your app built (Figure 13.2):

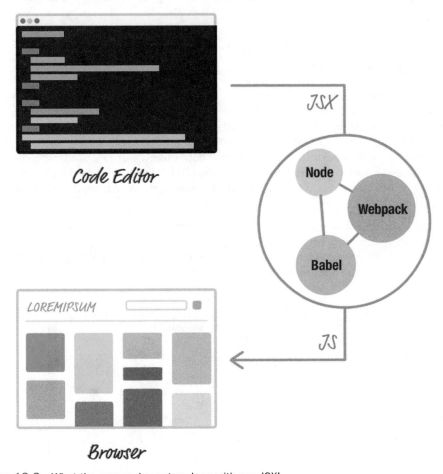

Figure 13.2   What the proper dev setup does with our JSX!

With this solution, your browser is loading your app and dealing with an already converted (and potentially optimized) JavaScript file. Good stuff, right? The only reason we delayed talking about all of this until now is for **simplicity**. Learning React is difficult enough. Adding the complexity of build tools and setting up your environment as part of learning React is just not cool. Now that you have a solid grasp of everything React does, it's time to change that with this chapter.

In the following sections, we're going to look at one way to set up your development environment using a combination of Node, Babel, and webpack. If all of this sounds bizarre to you, don't worry. We'll use a really nifty solution created by Facebook that makes all of this a breeze.

Onward!

Meet Create React

A few years ago, getting your build environment set up would have been a huge pain because it involved manually configuring all the tools we've talked about. You would have had to ask your really smart friend for some advice. You might even have questioned your decision to learn programming and React in the first place. Fortunately, the Create React project (https://github.com/facebookincubator/create-react-app) came about and greatly simplified the process of setting up your React environment. You just run a few commands on your command line, and your React project is automatically created with all the proper behind-the-scenes configurations.

To get started, first make sure you have the latest version of Node installed (https://nodejs.org/). Then bring up your favorite command line. If you aren't too familiar with command lines, don't worry. On Windows, launch either the command prompt or the BASH shell. On Mac, launch the Terminal. You'll see something that looks like this:

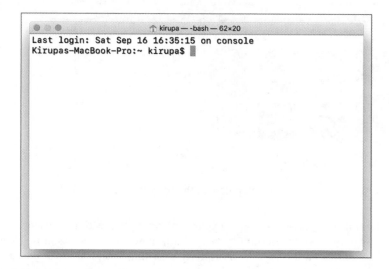

It's basically some bizarre window with a blinking cursor that allows you to type things into it. The first thing you need to do is install the Create React project. Type the following in your command line and press Enter/Return:

```
npm install -g create-react-app
```

It can take anywhere from a few seconds to a few minutes, but once your installation has completed, it's time to create our new React project. Navigate to the folder where you want to create your new project—this can be your desktop, a location under Documents, and so on. When you've navigated to a folder in your command line, enter the following to create a new project at this location:

```
create-react-app helloworld
```

You'll see something that looks as follows:

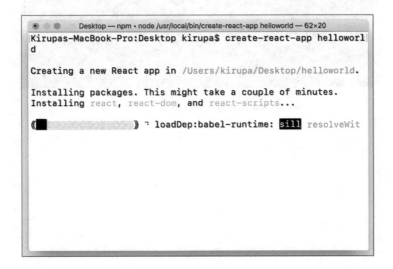

After the command has fully executed, you'll have a project called **helloworld** created for you. Don't worry too much about everything that's going on; we'll look at the project contents later. For now, the first thing to do is test this project. Navigate into the newly created project's `helloworld` folder by typing the following:

```
cd helloworld
```

From inside this folder, enter the following to test the app:

```
npm start
```

If you have yarn installed, Create will prefer it over npm for the install and you'll see onscreen instructions saying to use `yarn start` instead of `npm start`.

Your project will get built, a local web server will get started, and you'll see your project running, similar to the following image:

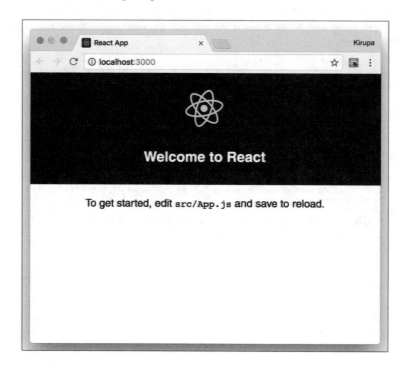

If everything worked out properly, you should see the same thing. If this is your first time creating a new React project using the command line, congratulations! This is a really big step. You aren't done, though. Now, we need to take a few steps back and revisit what exactly just happened.

Making Sense of What Happened

Right now, we just see whatever default content the `create-react-app` command generated for us. That isn't very helpful. First, let's take a look at what exactly gets generated. Your file and folder structure after running `create-react-app helloworld` will look as in Figure 13.3:

Figure 13.3   What our file and folder structure looks like.

The `index.html` in your `public` folder gets loaded in your browser. If you take a look at this file, you'll realize that it's very basic. Here are the contents of this file with all the comments removed:

```
<!DOCTYPE html>
<html>
  <head>
    <meta charset="utf-8">
    <meta name="viewport" content="width=device-width, initial-scale=1,
shrink-to-fit=no">
    <meta name="theme-color" content="#000000">

    <link rel="manifest" href="%PUBLIC_URL%/manifest.json">
    <link rel="shortcut icon" href="%PUBLIC_URL%/favicon.ico">

    <title>React App</title>
  </head>
  <body>
    <noscript>
      You need to enable JavaScript to run this app.
    </noscript>

    <div id="root"></div>

  </body>
</html>
```

The important part to look at is the `div` element with an `id` value of `root`. This is where the contents of our React app ultimately get printed to. Speaking of that, the contents of our React app with all the JSX are contained inside the `src` folder. The starting point for our React app is contained in `index.js`:

```
import React from 'react';
import ReactDOM from 'react-dom';
import './index.css';
import App from './App';
import registerServiceWorker from './registerServiceWorker';

ReactDOM.render(<App />, document.getElementById('root'));
registerServiceWorker();
```

Notice the `ReactDOM.render` call that looks for the `root` element we called out inside `index.html`. You'll also see a bunch of `import` statements at the top of the page. These `import` statements are part of something in JavaScript known as **modules**. The goal of modules is to divide the functionality of your app into increasingly smaller pieces. When it comes time to use a piece, you import only what you need instead of everything and the entire kitchen sink. Some of the modules you import are a part of code in your project. Other modules, like `React` and `ReactDOM`, are external to your project but still capable of being imported. I can say a lot about module loading, but for your sanity (and mine!), let's just leave that topic alone for now.

In our code right now, we're importing both the React and React-DOM libraries. That should be familiar from when we included the script tags for them earlier. We're also importing a CSS file, a service worker script that we'll reference as `registerServiceWorker`, and a React component that we'll reference as `App`.

Our `App` component seems like our next stop, so to see what's inside it, open `App.js`:

```
import React, { Component } from 'react';
import logo from './logo.svg';
import './App.css';

class App extends Component {
  render() {
    return (
      <div className="App">
        <header className="App-header">
          <img src={logo} className="App-logo" alt="logo" />
          <h1 className="App-title">Welcome to React</h1>
        </header>
        <p className="App-intro">
          To get started, edit <code>src/App.js</code> and save to reload.
        </p>
      </div>
    );
  }
}

export default App;
```

Notice that our `App.js` file has `import` statements of its own. Some, such as the one for React and Component, seem necessary, given what our code is doing. The last line here is interesting: `export default app`. It contains the `export` command and the name that our project will use to identify the exported module. You'll use this exported name when importing the App module in other parts of the project, such as `index.js`. Closing out what this file is doing, it also imports an image and CSS file that are needed to make this page work.

You've now seen a different way of structuring code using some potentially new keywords. What's the purpose of all of this? These modules, `import` statements, and `export` statements are just niceties to make our app's code more manageable. Instead of having everything defined in one giant file, you can break your code and related assets across multiple files. Depending on which files you reference and what files get loaded ahead of other files, our mysterious build process (currently kicked off with an `npm start`) can optimize the final output in a variety of ways that we don't need to worry about.

The important point to note is that none of these things you are doing to your code affect the functionality of your final app in any major way. Behind the scenes, when we're ready to test our app, a build step takes place. This build step makes sense of all of the various files and components you are importing, to present them as an easily digestible set of combined files for the browser to take care of. We'll get one JS file with all the relevant pieces represented:

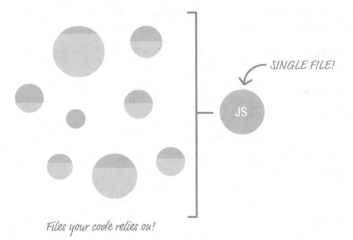

Files your code relies on!

We'll also get one combined CSS file. Depending on what else you might have configured, you could get other combined files for your HTML and more. All of these will be in a form that your browser will immediately know what to do with. Your browser will have no additional work to do, as in our in-browser solution we were using initially. Everything gets generated as vanilla HTML, CSS, and JavaScript.

Creating Our HelloWorld App

Now that you've gotten a better idea of what this project is doing, let's modify the example. We want to display the words Hello, world! to our screen. We'll go about this by creating a component, appropriately called HelloWorld, to handle it for us. The new part in this isn't that you get some text to display onscreen; you're a pro at that by this point. The part to focus on is how to structure the files in your project to ensure that you're creating your app the *right* way.

To get started, go to your src directory and delete all the files you see there. Then create a new file called index.js. Inside that file, add the following contents:

```
import React from "react";
import ReactDOM from "react-dom";
import HelloWorld from "./HelloWorld";

ReactDOM.render(
    <HelloWorld/>,
    document.getElementById("root")
);
```

We're importing our React and ReactDOM modules here. We're also importing a component called HelloWorld that we are specifying in our ReactDOM.render call. That component doesn't exist, so we are going to fix that next.

In the same src directory that we're in right now, create a file called HelloWorld.js. Then go ahead and modify it by adding in the following:

```
import React, { Component } from "react";

class HelloWorld extends Component {
  render() {
    return (
      <div className="helloContainer">
        <h1>Hello, world!</h1>
      </div>
    );
  }
}


export default HelloWorld;
```

Take a moment to look through what you've added. You shouldn't see anything really exciting going on here—just a boring import statement, our HelloWorld component that prints some text to the screen, and (in the last line) code that tags our HelloWorld component for exporting so that it can be imported by another module, such as our index.js.

With these changes made, we can test the application. Make sure you've saved all your changes. Go back to the command line and type in npm start. If your app was already running behind the scenes, you would automatically see it update with the latest changes. If that didn't happen or your app stopped, press Ctrl+C to stop the session and enter npm start again.

You should see something similar to this on your screen:

If this is what you see, great! Our example is working now, but it looks a little too plain. Let's fix that by adding some CSS. Create a stylesheet called index.css, and add the following style rule into it:

```css
body {
  display: flex;
  align-items: center;
  justify-content: center;
  min-height: 100vh;
  margin: 0;
}
```

In this approach for building apps, creating the stylesheet is only one part of what you have to do. The other part requires you to reference the newly created index.css in the index.js file. Open index.js and add the highlighted import statement for it:

```js
import React from "react";
import ReactDOM from "react-dom";
import HelloWorld from "./HelloWorld";
import "./index.css";

ReactDOM.render(
    <HelloWorld/>,
    document.getElementById("root")
);
```

If you go back to your browser, you'll notice that the current setup automatically refreshes your page with all the latest changes. You'll see the words `Hello, world!` centered vertically and horizontally for you. Not bad, but we can do better.

The last thing we want to do is make our text appear in a more stylish fashion. We could add the appropriate style rules to `index.css` itself, but the more appropriate solution is to create a new CSS file that we reference only in our `HelloWorld` component. The end result of both approaches is identical, but you want to get into the practice of grouping related files (and their dependencies) together, as part of being a better developer.

Create a new file called `HelloWorld.css` inside the `src` folder. Add the following style rule into it:

```css
h1 {
    font-family: sans-serif;
    font-size: 56px;
    padding: 5px;
    padding-left: 15px;
    padding-right: 15px;
    margin: 0;
    background: linear-gradient(to bottom,
                                white 0%,
                                white 62%,
                                gold 62%,
                                gold 100%);
}
```

All that's left is to reference this stylesheet in the `HelloWorld.js` file, so open that file and add the highlighted `import` statement:

```js
import React, { Component } from "react";
import "./HelloWorld.css";

class HelloWorld extends Component {
  render() {
    return (
      <div className="helloContainer">
        <h1>Hello, world!</h1>
      </div>
    );
  }
}

export default HelloWorld;
```

If you go back to your browser, you know that everything worked out fine if you see something like the following:

You'll see the words Hello, world! displayed, but with a little more style and pizazz (as the cool kids say these days) than they did a few moments ago.

Creating a Production Build

We're almost done. We've got just one more thing left to do. So far, we've been building this app in **development mode**. In this mode, our code isn't minified and some of the things run in a slow/verbose setting so that we can debug issues more easily. When it's time to send the app live to our real users, we want the fastest and most compact solution possible. For that, we can go back to the command line and enter the following (after stopping the build by pressing Ctrl+C):

```
npm run build
```

The script takes a few minutes to create an optimized set of files for you. Once it has run to completion, you'll see some confirmation text that looks as follows:

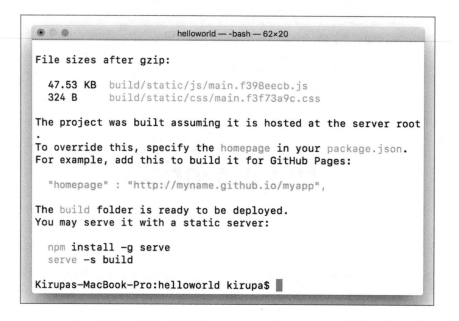

When this has completed, you can follow the onscreen prompts to deploy it to your server or just test it locally using the popular `serve` node package.

Also take a moment to browse through all the files that were generated. The end result is just plain HTML, CSS, and JS files. No JSX. No multiple JS files. We have just a single JS file that contains all the logic our app needs to work.

Conclusion

So that just happened! In the preceding sections, we used the awesome Create React solution to create our React app in a modern way. If this is your first time building apps like this, you'll want to get more familiar with this approach. We use the `create-react-app` command for future React examples; our earlier in-browser approach was just to help you learn the basics without fiddling with all of what you saw here. Under the covers, Create React hides a lot of the complexity that goes with tweaking Node, Babel, webpack, and other components. That is its greatest strength, as well as its greatest weakness.

If you want to go beyond the happy path that Create React provides, you'll need to learn a lot of the complexity hidden underneath. Covering all of that goes beyond this book. As a starting point, take a look at what's specified in the various JS files under the `node_modules/react_scripts/scripts` path.

> ### Note: If you run into any issues, ask!
>
> If you have any questions or your code isn't running like you expect, don't hesitate to ask! Post on the forums at https://forum.kirupa.com and get help from some of the friendliest and most knowledgeable people the Internet has ever brought together!

14

Working with External Data in React

Dealing with external data is pretty much standard in web apps today. This "dealing" typically looks as follows:

1. Your app makes a request for some data to a remote service.

2. The remote service receives the request and sends back some data.

3. Your app receives the data.

4. Your app formats and displays the data to the user.

Whether or not you realize it, almost all your favorite websites follow these four steps...Facebook, Amazon, Twitter, Instagram, Gmail, KIRUPA, and so on. When you starting loading a page on any of these sites, they all display some data initially.

To keep your initial page size low, not everything is downloaded at once. After your page has fully loaded or you interact with your page, the page downloads additional data from the server and displays it.

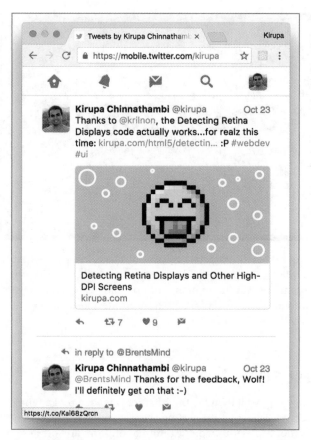

This is all done without requiring you to refresh the page or lose any state your page is in. The magic behind it all is a little bit of JavaScript that handles the four steps we looked at earlier. In this chapter, you'll learn all about the JavaScript needed to do that and how to make it all work inside a React app.

By the end, you'll have created a simple React app that looks as follows (view in your browser here: https://www.kirupa.com/react/examples/ipaddress.htm):

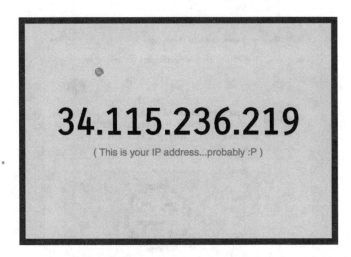

Here you're seeing your device's IP address displayed. That's it. I realize that this isn't very complicated, as examples go (especially if you were all excited seeing Twitter highlighted in the screenshots), but it contains just the right amount of complexity and relevant details to ensure that you know how to deal with external data from inside a React app.

Onward!

Web Request 101

As you probably know very well by now, the Internet is made up of a bunch of interconnected computers, called servers. When you're surfing the web and navigating between web pages, you're really telling your browser to request information from any of these servers. It kind of looks as follows: Your browser sends a request, waits awkwardly for the server to respond to the request, and (once the server responds) processes the request. All of this communication is made possible because of something known as the **HTTP protocol**.

The HTTP protocol provides a common language that allows your browser and a bunch of other things to communicate with all the servers that make up the Internet. The requests your browser makes on your behalf using the HTTP protocol are known as **HTTP requests**, and these requests go well beyond simply loading a new page as you are navigating. A common (and whole lot more exciting!) set of use cases revolves around updating your *existing* page with data resulting from a HTTP request.

For example, you might have a page where you'd like to display some information about the currently logged-in user. This is information your page might not have initially, but it is information your browser will request when you're interacting with the page. The server will respond with the data and update your page with that information. All of this probably sounds a bit abstract, so I'm going to go a bit weird for a few moments and describe a possible HTTP request and response for this example.

To get information about the user, here's our HTTP request:

```
GET /user
Accept: application/json
```

For that request, here's what the server might return:

```
200 OK
Content-Type: application/json

{
  "name": "Kirupa",
  "url": "http:https://www.kirupa.com"
}
```

This back-and-forth happens a bunch of times, and it's all fully supported in JavaScript. This ability to asynchronously request and process data from a server without requiring a page navigation/reload has a term: **Ajax** (or **AJAX**, if you want to shout). This acronym stands for Asynchronous JavaScript and XML. If you were around web developers a few years ago, Ajax was the buzzword everybody threw around to describe the kind of web apps we take for granted today (Twitter, Facebook, Google Maps, Gmail, and more) that constantly fetch data as you interact with the page, without requiring a full page reload.

In JavaScript, the object that is responsible for allowing you to send and receive HTTP requests is the weirdly named XMLHttpRequest. This object allows you to do several things that are important to making web requests:

1. Send a request to a server

2. Check on the status of a request

3. Retrieve and parse the response from the request

4. Listen for the readystatechange event that helps you react to the status of your request

XMLHttpRequest does a few more things, but those aren't important to deal with right now.

Why Not Use Third-Party Libraries?

A bunch of third-party libraries wrap and simplify how you can work with the XMLHttpRequest object. Feel free to use them if you want, but using the XMLHttpRequest object directly isn't very complicated, either. It's only a few lines of code, and (compared to everything you've been learning in React) they're some of the easiest lines of code you'll encounter.

It's React Time!

Now that you have a good enough understanding of how HTTP requests and the XMLHttpRequest object work, it's time to shift our focus to the React side. I should warn you, though, that React brings very little to the table when it comes to working with external data. React is primarily focused on the presentation layer (a.k.a. the V in MVC). We'll be writing regular, boring JavaScript inside *a React component whose primary purpose is to deal with the web requests we'll be making*. We'll talk more about that design choice in a little bit, but let's get the example up and running first.

Getting Started

The first step is to create a new React app. From your command line, navigate to the folder where you want to create your new project and enter the following:

```
create-react-app ipaddress
```

Press Enter/Return to run that command. A few moments later, a brand new React project will be created. You want to start from a blank slate, so you're going to delete a lot of things. First, delete everything under your `public` folder. Next, delete everything inside your `src` folder. Don't worry: You'll fill them back with content you care about in a few moments, starting with your HTML file.

Inside the `public` folder, create a new file called `index.html`. Add the following content into it:

```html
<!DOCTYPE html>
<html>

<head>
  <title>IP Address</title>
</head>

<body>
  <div id="container">

  </div>
</body>

</html>
```

All we have going here is a `div` element named `container`. Next, go to your `src` folder and create a new file called `index.js`. Inside this file, add the following:

```js
import React from "react";
import ReactDOM from "react-dom";
import "./index.css";
import IPAddressContainer from "./IPAddressContainer";

var destination = document.querySelector("#container");

ReactDOM.render(
    <div>
        <IPAddressContainer/>
    </div>,
    destination
);
```

This is the script entry point for our app, and it contains the boilerplate references to React, ReactDOM, a nonexistent CSS file, and a nonexistent `IPAddressContainer` component. We also have the `ReactDOM.render` call that is responsible for writing our content to the `container` `div` element we defined in our HTML a few moments ago.

There's just one more thing to do before we get to the really interesting stuff. Inside the `src` folder, create the `index.css` file and add the following style rule into it:

```css
body {
  background-color: #FFCC00;
}
```

Save all these changes if you haven't done so already. We sort of have the beginnings of our app started. In the next section, we're going to make our app really useful—or at least get really close!

Getting the IP Address

Next on our plate is to create a component whose job it is to fetch the IP address from a web service, store it as **state**, and then share that state as a **prop** to any component that requires it. Let's create a component to help. Inside your `src` folder, add a file called `IPAddressContainer.js` and then add the following lines inside it:

```js
import React, { Component } from "react";

class IPAddressContainer extends Component {
  render() {
    return (
      <p>Nothing yet!</p>
    );
  }
}


export default IPAddressContainer;
```

The lines you just added don't do a whole lot. They just print the words `Nothing yet!` to the screen. That's not bad for now, but let's go ahead and modify the code to make the HTTP request by adding the following changes:

```js
var xhr;

class IPAddressContainer extends Component {
  constructor(props) {
    super(props);

    this.state = {
      ip_address: "..."
    };

    this.processRequest = this.processRequest.bind(this);
  }
```

```
componentDidMount() {
  xhr = new XMLHttpRequest();
  xhr.open("GET", "https://ipinfo.io/json", true);
  xhr.send();

  xhr.addEventListener("readystatechange", this.processRequest, false);
}

processRequest() {
  if (xhr.readyState === 4 && xhr.status === 200) {
    var response = JSON.parse(xhr.responseText);

    this.setState({
      ip_address: response.ip
    });
  }
}

render() {
  return (
    <div>Nothing yet!</div>
  );
}
};
```

Now we're getting somewhere! When our component becomes active and the component-
DidMount lifecycle method gets called, we make our HTTP request and send it off to the
ipinfo.io web service:

```
        .
        .
        .
      componentDidMount() {
        xhr = new XMLHttpRequest();
        xhr.open('GET', "https://ipinfo.io/json", true);
        xhr.send();

        xhr.addEventListener("readystatechange", this.processRequest, false);
      }
        .
        .
        .
```

When we hear a response back from the `ipinfo` service, we call the `processRequest` function to help us deal with the result:

```
      .
      .
      .
  processRequest() {
    if (xhr.readyState === 4 && xhr.status === 200) {
      var response = JSON.parse(xhr.responseText);

      this.setState({
        ip_address: response.ip
      });
    }
      .
      .
      .
```

Next, modify the `render` call to reference the IP address value stored by our state:

```
var xhr;

class IPAddressContainer extends Component {
  constructor(props) {
    super(props);

    this.state = {
      ip_address: "..."
    };

    this.processRequest = this.processRequest.bind(this);
  }

  componentDidMount() {
    xhr = new XMLHttpRequest();
    xhr.open("GET", "https://ipinfo.io/json", true);
    xhr.send();

    xhr.addEventListener("readystatechange", this.processRequest, false);
  }

  processRequest() {
    if (xhr.readyState === 4 && xhr.status === 200) {
      var response = JSON.parse(xhr.responseText);
```

```
      this.setState({
        ip_address: response.ip
      });
    }
  }

  render() {
    return (
      <div>{this.state.ip_address}</div>
    );
  }
}
```

If you preview your app in your browser, you should see an IP address displayed. If you need a reminder, you can preview your app by navigating into your `ipaddress` folder via your command line and entering `npm start`. When your app launches, it will look something like the following:

Our app currently doesn't look like much, but we'll fix that in the next section.

Kicking the Visuals Up a Notch

The hard part is done! We created a component that handles all the HTTP requesting shenanigans, and we know that it returns the IP address when called. Now we're going to format the output a bit so that it doesn't look as plain as it does now.

To do that, we won't add HTML elements and styling-related details to our IPAddressContainer component's render method. Instead, we'll create a new component whose only purpose will be to deal with all of that.

Add a new file called IPAddress.js in your src folder. Then edit it by adding the following content into it:

```
import React, { Component } from "react";

class IPAddress extends Component {
  render() {
    return (
      <div>
        Blah!
      </div>
    );
  }
}

export default IPAddress;
```

Here we're defining a new component called IPAddress that will be responsible for displaying the additional text and ensuring that our IP address is visually formatted exactly the way we want. It doesn't do much right now, but that will change really quickly.

We first want to modify this component's render method to look as follows:

```
class IPAddress extends Component {
  render() {
    return (
      <div>
        <h1>{this.props.ip}</h1>
        <p>( This is your IP address...probably :P )</p>
      </div>
    );
  }
}

export default IPAddress;
```

The highlighted changes should be self-explanatory. We're putting the results of a prop value called ip inside an h1 tag, and we're displaying some additional text using a p tag. Besides making the rendered HTML a bit more semantic, these changes ensure that we can style them better.

To get these elements styled, add a new CSS file to the src folder called IPAddress.css. Inside this file, add the following style rules:

```
h1 {
  font-family: sans-serif;
  text-align: center;
```

```
  padding-top: 140px;
  font-size: 60px;
  margin: -15px;
}
p {
  font-family: sans-serif;
  color: #907400;
  text-align: center;
}
```

With the styles defined, we need to reference this CSS file in our `IPAddress.js` file. To do that, add the following highlighted line:

```
import React, { Component } from "react";
import "./IPAddress.css";

class IPAddress extends Component {
  render() {
    return (
      <div>
        <h1>{this.props.ip}</h1>
        <p>( This is your IP address...probably :P )</p>
      </div>
    );
  }
}


export default IPAddress;
```

All that remains is to use our `IPAddress` component and pass in the IP address. The first step is to ensure that the `IPAddressContainer` component is aware of the `IPAddress` component by referencing it. At the top of `IPAddressContainer.js`, add the following highlighted line:

```
import React, { Component } from "react";
import IPAddress from "./IPAddress";
  .
  .
  .
```

The second (and last!) step is to modify the `render` method as follows:

```
class IPAddressContainer extends Component {
  .
  .
  .
  render() {
    return (
      <IPAddress ip={this.state.ip_address}/>
    );
  }
}
```

In our highlighted line, we call our IPAddress component, define a prop called ip, and set its value to the ip_address state variable. This is done to ensure that our IP address value travels all the way back to the IPAddress component's render method, where it gets formatted and displayed.

If you preview the app in your browser now, you should see something identical to the example we set out to create in the beginning.

At this point, you're done with the app...and almost done with this tutorial. You just need to know one more thing about these awesome components that you've added.

Presentational vs. Container Components

Given what we've seen here so far, it seems like a good time to talk about a design choice that we've been indirectly following not just in this tutorial, but in other tutorials as well. In our React apps, we have been primarily dealing with two types of components:

1. **Components that deal with how things look.** These are better known as presentational components.

2. **Components that perform some under-the-covers processing.** Examples of this processing include routing, increasing a counter, fetching data via a HTTP request, and so on. You will see these components referred to as container components.

Thinking about your components in terms of whether they display something (presentational) or whether they feed data to other components (container) helps you better organize your React app. For the full low-down on how to deal with these two types of components, check out this article by React's Dan Abramov: https://medium.com/@dan_abramov/smart-and-dumb-components-7ca2f9a7c7d0.

Conclusion

At this point, you're probably wondering what was made special because of React. All we really did here was use a boring old JavaScript API inside a component, hook up some events, and do the same state- and prop-related tasks you've done several times already. Here's the thing: You've already learned almost everything there is to learn about the basics of React. Going forward, nothing should surprise you. The only new things we'll be looking at fall into the category of repurposing and repackaging the basic concepts you already know into newer and cooler situations. After all, isn't that what programming is all about?

Note: If you run into any issues, ask!

If you have any questions or your code isn't running like you expect, don't hesitate to ask! Post on the forums at https://forum.kirupa.com and get help from some of the friendliest and most knowledgeable people the Internet has ever brought together!

15

Building an Awesome Todo List App in React

If creating the Hello, World! example was a celebration of getting your feet wet with React, creating the quintessential Todo List app is a celebration of approaching React mastery. In this chapter, we tie together a lot of the concepts and techniques you've learned to create something that works as follows: https://www.kirupa.com/react/examples/todo.htm.

You start with a blank app that allows you to enter tasks for later (see Figure 15.1).

Figure 15.1   A blank app with task entry.

The way this Todo List app works is pretty simple. You type in a task or item or whatever you want into the input field and then press Add (or click Enter/Return). After you've submitted your item, you'll see it appear as an entry. You can keep adding items and have them all show up (see Figure 15.2).

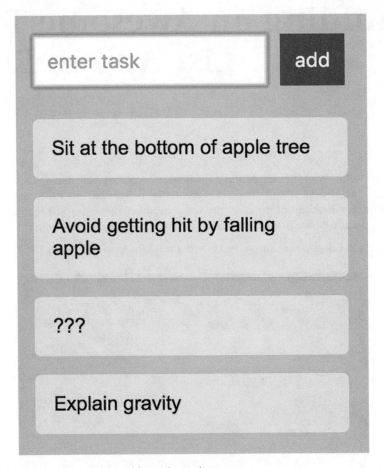

Figure 15.2 You can add tasks and have them show up.

To remove an item, just click on an existing entry. Pretty simple, right? In the following sections, we build this app together from scratch using a lot of the adrenaline-inducing techniques you've learned so far.

Chemical structure for
Adrenaline (aka Epinephrine)

This is going to be a fun exercise of building each part of the app and learning (in awesomely painstaking detail) how the various little things work along the way.

Onward!

Getting Started

The first step is to create a new React app, as you learned in Chapter 13, "Setting Up Your React Dev Environment Easily." From your command line, navigate to the folder where you want to create your new project and enter the following:

```
create-react-app todolist
```

Press Enter/Return to run that command. A few moments later, a brand new React project is created. We want to start from a blank slate, so we're going to delete everything contained in our `public` folder and our `src` folder.

By now, you know the drill. You need a starting point, so go ahead and create a new HTML document inside your `public` folder called `index.html`. Inside it, add the following content:

```
<!DOCTYPE html>
<html>

<head>
  <title>Todo List</title>
</head>
```

```
<body>
  <div id="container">

  </div>
</body>

</html>
```

This page is pretty basic, as you can tell. The real magic is going to be happening in the src directory, where your JavaScript and CSS files will live. In the src directory, create a new file called index.css and add the following style rules into it:

```
body {
  padding: 50px;
  background-color: #66CCFF;
  font-family: sans-serif;
}
#container {
  display: flex;
  justify-content: center;
}
```

Now let's add the JavaScript that rounds out the starting page. Within the same src directory, add a new file called index.js. Inside this file, add the following content:

```
import React from "react";
import ReactDOM from "react-dom";
import "./index.css";

var destination = document.querySelector("#container");

ReactDOM.render(
    <div>
        <p>Hello!</p>
    </div>,
    destination
);
```

Take a moment to look at what you've just added. By now, you should be fully familiar with what's going on with the HTML, CSS, and JavaScript here. What we really have is the foundation. In the following sections, we'll build on top of this all the pieces that make up the rest of our Todo List app.

Creating the Initial UI

Right now, our app doesn't do a whole lot. It doesn't look like much, either. We'll deal with the functionality in a little bit, but first let's get the various UI elements up and running. That isn't very complicated for our app. First we'll get our input field and button to appear. This is all done by using the div, form, input, and button elements.

All of that will live inside a component we'll call `TodoList`. In your `src` folder, add a file called `TodoList.js`. Inside this file, add the following:

```
import React, { Component } from "react";

class TodoList extends Component {
  render() {
    return (
      <div className="todoListMain">
        <div className="header">
          <form>
            <input placeholder="enter task">
            </input>
            <button type="submit">add</button>
          </form>
        </div>
      </div>
    );
  }
}

export default TodoList;
```

Take a moment to glance at what you've added. You can see a bunch of JSX that gets the form elements up and running. To use the newly created `TodoList` component, let's go back to `index.js` and reference it to see how our app looks now. Go ahead and make the following two changes:

```
import React from "react";
import ReactDOM from "react-dom";
import "./index.css";
import TodoList from "./TodoList";

var destination = document.querySelector("#container");

ReactDOM.render(
    <div>
        <TodoList/>
    </div>,
    destination
);
```

Save all your changes and preview in your browser. If everything worked, you'll see something that looks like Figure 15.3.

Figure 15.3   What our app looks like right now.

Right now, we have our input field and submit button showing up. These two UI elements neither work nor look too visually appealing. We'll fix that in a little bit, but first let's talk about how we're going to add the rest of the app's functionality.

Building the Rest of the App

As you can imagine, getting the initial UI elements to show up is the easy part. Tying up all the visuals with the underlying data is where the real work lies. This work can roughly be divided into five parts:

1. Adding items

2. Displaying items

3. Styling

4. Removing items

5. Animating items as they are added or removed

Individually, all of these little implementation details are easy to wrap your brain around. When you put them together, you need to watch out for a few things. We'll look at all that and more in the following sections.

Adding Items

The first major task to tackle is setting up the event handlers and default form-handling behavior to allow us to add an item. Go back to the `form` element and make the following highlighted change:

```
class TodoList extends Component {
  render() {
    return (
      <div className="todoListMain">
        <div className="header">
          <form onSubmit={this.addItem}>
            <input placeholder="enter task">
            </input>
            <button type="submit">add</button>
          </form>
        </div>
      </div>
    );
  }
}
```

We listen for the `submit` event on the form itself, and we call the `addItem` method when that event is overheard. Notice that we aren't listening for any event on the button itself. This is because our button has a `type` attribute set to `submit`. This is one of those HTML trickeries in which clicking on the button whose `type` is `submit` is the equivalent of firing the `submit` event on the form.

Now it's time to create our `addItem` event handler that will get called when our form gets submitted. Add the following highlighted lines just above where we have our `render` function defined:

```
class TodoList extends Component {
  constructor(props) {
    super(props);

    this.addItem = this.addItem.bind(this);
  }

  addItem(e) {

  }
  .
  .
  .
}
```

All we did was define our `addItem` event handler and ensure that the keyword resolves properly. We still haven't done anything remotely close to actually adding a task, so let's start by first defining our `state` object in the constructor:

```
constructor(props) {
  super(props);

  this.state = {
    items: []
  };

  this.addItem = this.addItem.bind(this);
}
```

Our `state` object isn't very complicated. We're just defining an items array/property that will be responsible for storing the various items that you can enter. All that's left to do now is read the entered value from our input element and store it in our `items` array when the user submits it. The only complication here is actually reading the value from a DOM element. As you know, React puts up a gate between us and the DOM. It doesn't like to have us accessing DOM elements and fiddling with properties on them, but it does give us a loophole via refs that we can use.

In our `render` function, make the following highlighted change:

```
render() {
  return (
    <div className="todoListMain">
      <div className="header">
        <form onSubmit={this.addItem}>
          <input ref={(a) => this._inputElement = a}
                 placeholder="enter task">
          </input>
          <button type="submit">add</button>
        </form>
      </div>
    </div>
  );
}
```

Here we're storing a reference to our `input` element in the appropriately named `_inputElement` property. To state this differently, anywhere inside this component where we want to access our `input` element, we can do so by accessing `_inputElement`. Now it's time to fill out our `addItem` function with the following content:

```
addItem(e) {
  var itemArray = this.state.items;

  if (this._inputElement.value !== "") {
    itemArray.unshift({
```

```
    text: this._inputElement.value,
    key: Date.now()
  });

  this.setState({
    items: itemArray
  });

  this._inputElement.value = "";
}

console.log(itemArray);

e.preventDefault();
}
```

Take a moment to look through what we're doing. We create a variable called `itemArray` to store the current value of our items `state` object. Next, we check to see if our input element has any content inside it. If it's empty, we don't do anything. If our input element has some text entered, we add that text to our `itemArray`:

```
itemArray.unshift({
  text: this._inputElement.value,
  key: Date.now()
});
```

We aren't just adding the entered text. We're actually adding an object that contains both the entered text and a unique key value that's set by the current time (`Date.now()`). If you aren't clear on why we're specifying the key, that's okay. You'll totally see why in a few moments.

The rest of our code is pretty boring. We're setting our state's `items` property to the value of `itemArray`. We're clearing the value of our `input` element to make room for the next todo item. This line here might be less boring:

```
e.preventDefault();
```

We're overriding this event's default behavior. The reason has to do with how form submission works. By default, when you submit a form, the page reloads and clears everything out. We definitely don't want that. By calling `preventDefault`, we block the default behavior. That's a good thing!

It's time to take stock of where we are right now. If you preview your app and check the browser console, you'll see our `state` object correctly populating with each new todo item we added (see Figure 15.4).

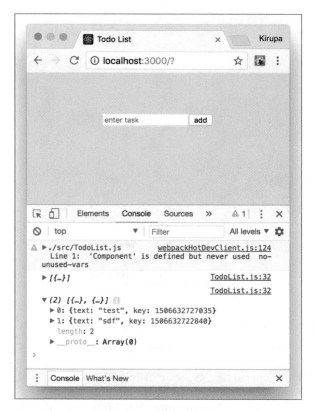

Figure 15.4 We can now see the entries being stored. I realize that this might not seem like much, but we're making great progress—seriously!

> **Note**
>
> For an alternate approach for setting new state inside the add. This method without modifying the existing state, check out this version: http://bit.ly/setStateConcat.

Displaying the Items

Having our todo items show up only in the console might be exciting for some of your users, but I'm pretty certain that most probably want to see these items displayed directly on the page. To do this, we're going to rely on another component. To get started, let's call this component `TodoItems`, specify it in our `TodoList` component's `render` method, and pass in our `items` array as a prop.

All of that translated into markup and code looks as follows:

```
render() {
  return (
    <div className="todoListMain">
      <div className="header">
        <form onSubmit={this.addItem}>
```

```
            <input ref={(a) => this._inputElement = a}
                    placeholder="enter task">
            </input>
            <button type="submit">add</button>
          </form>
        </div>
        <TodoItems entries={this.state.items}/>
      </div>
    );
}
```

After you've done this, add the `import` statement to the top of the document as well:

```
import React, { Component } from "react";
import TodoItems from "./TodoItems";

class TodoList extends Component {
  .
  .
  .
```

These two changes wrap up the work we want to do in `TodoList.js` for now. Next, let's go ahead and *actually* create our `TodoItems` component. In the `src` directory, create a new file called `TodoItems.js` and add the following content into it:

```
import React, { Component } from "react";

class TodoItems extends Component {
  constructor(props) {
    super(props);

    this.createTasks = this.createTasks.bind(this);
  }

  createTasks(item) {
    return <li key={item.key}>{item.text}</li>
  }

  render() {
    var todoEntries = this.props.entries;
    var listItems = todoEntries.map(this.createTasks);

    return (
      <ul className="theList">
        {listItems}
      </ul>
    );
  }
};

export default TodoItems;
```

This might look like a lot of code to add in one giant swoop, but take a moment to look at what exactly you're adding. In our `render` function, we're taking the list of todo items (passed in as entries) and turning them into JSX/HTML-ish elements. We do that by calling `map` on our items and relying on the `createTasks` function:

```
createTasks(item) {
  return <li key={item.key}>{item.text}</li>
}
```

The value stored by our `listItems` variable is an array of `li` elements that contain the appropriate content to print. Notice that we're setting the `key` attribute—whose value, as you recall, we set earlier using `Date.now()`—on each element, to make it easier for React to keep track of the elements.

We turn this list of elements into something we can show onscreen with the following:

```
return (
  <ul className="theList">
    {listItems}
  </ul>
);
```

After you've made this change, save all the changes and preview the app in its current state (`npm start` if it isn't already running). If everything worked properly, not only will you be able to add items, but you also will be able to see them (see Figure 15.5).

Figure 15.5   Our entries are now showing up!

If what you see looks similar to the figure, that's awesome! To celebrate, let's take a little break from looking at JS and JSX.

Styling our App

Right now, our app's awesome functionality isn't reflected in how the app currently looks. We're going to fix this easily by adding one stylesheet and putting all the relevant style rules into it. In the `src` folder, create a new stylesheet called `TodoList.css` and add the following style rules into it:

```css
.todoListMain .header input {
  padding: 10px;
  font-size: 16px;
  border: 2px solid #FFF;
  width: 165px;
}
.todoListMain .header button {
  padding: 10px;
  font-size: 16px;
  margin: 10px;
  margin-right: 0px;
  background-color: #0066FF;
  color: #FFF;
  border: 2px solid #0066FF;
}
.todoListMain .header button:hover {
  background-color: #003399;
  border: 2px solid #003399;
  cursor: pointer;
}
.todoListMain .theList {
  list-style: none;
  padding-left: 0;
  width: 250px;
}
.todoListMain .theList li {
  color: #333;
  background-color: rgba(255,255,255,.5);
  padding: 15px;
  margin-bottom: 15px;
  border-radius: 5px;
}
```

After you've created this stylesheet, you need to reference it. In `TodoList.js`, add a reference to this stylesheet at the top:

```js
import React, { Component } from "react";
```

```
import TodoItems from "./TodoItems";
import "./TodoList.css";

class TodoList extends Component {
    .
    .
    .
```

If you preview your app after this change, it will look as shown in Figure 15.6.

Figure 15.6   Our app is starting to look much nicer.

As you can see, our app looks much nicer. All we did is add some CSS, so from a functionality point of view, nothing has changed. We'll make more progress on functionality next.

Removing Items

At this point, we can add items and see them appear. What we can't do is remove items after they've been added. We're going to allow users to remove items by clicking on them directly. This seems straightforward to implement, right? The only thing to watch out for involves where to put all our code. The items we click on are defined in `TodoItems.js`. The actual logic for populating the items lives in our `state` object in `TodoList.js`. To give you a preview of what to expect, we will be partaking in some shenanigans as we pass things between both of those components.

First we need to set up the event handler for dealing with the `click` event. Change the `return` statement under `createTasks` to look as follows:

```
createTasks(item) {
  return <li onClick={() => this.delete(item.key)}
          key={item.key}>{item.text}</li>
}
```

We're simply listening to the `click` event and associating it with an event handler called `delete`. What might be new is our approach for passing arguments to the event handler. Because of how event arguments and event handlers deal with scope, we work around all those issues using an `arrow` function that allows us both to maintain the default event argument and pass in our own arguments. If this seems bizarre, you can feel better knowing that this is a JavaScript quirk and has nothing to do with React.

After you've made this change, you need to define the `delete` event handler. Make the following highlighted changes:

```
class TodoItems extends Component {
  constructor(props) {
    super(props);

    this.createTasks = this.createTasks.bind(this);
  }

  delete(key) {
    this.props.delete(key);
  }
  .
  .
  .
```

Here we define a function called `delete` that takes our argument for the item key. To ensure that this resolves properly, we explicitly bind this in the constructor. Notice that our `delete` function doesn't actually do any deleting. It just calls *another* `delete` function passed into this component via props. We'll work backward from here and deal with that next.

In `TodoList.js`, take a look at our `render` function. When calling `TodoItems`, let's specify a prop called `delete` and set it to the value of a function called `deleteItem`:

```
render() {
  return (
    <div className="todoListMain">
      <div className="header">
        <form onSubmit={this.addItem}>
          <input ref={(a) => this._inputElement = a}
                 placeholder="enter task">
          </input>
          <button type="submit">add</button>
        </form>
      </div>
      <TodoItems entries={this.state.items}
                 delete={this.deleteItem}/>
    </div>
  );
}
```

This change ensures that our `TodoItems` component now has knowledge of a prop called `delete`. This also means that our `delete` function we added in `TodoList` actually connects. All that remains is actually defining our `deleteItem` function so that it can deal with deleting an item.

First, go ahead and add the `deleteItem` function to your `TodoList` component:

```
deleteItem(key) {
  var filteredItems = this.state.items.filter(function(item) {
    return (item.key !== key);
  });

  this.setState({
    items: filteredItems
  });
}
```

You can add it anywhere, but my preference is to put it just below where our `addItem` function lives. Take a look at what this code does. We are passing the key from our clicked item all the way here, and we check this key against all the items we're storing currently via the `filter` method:

```
var filteredItems = this.state.items.filter(function(item) {
  return (item.key !== key);
});
```

The result of running this code is simple. We create a new array called `filteredItems` that contains everything except the item we are removing. This filtered array is then set as our new `items` property on our `state` object:

```
this.setState({
  items: filteredItems
});
```

Our UI then updates and the removed item disappears forever. The last thing we need to do is deal with the usual shenanigans surrounding this. Make the following change in the constructor:

```
constructor(props) {
  super(props);

  this.state = {
    items: []
  };

  this.addItem = this.addItem.bind(this);
  this.deleteItem = this.deleteItem.bind(this);
}
```

This ensures that all references to this inside `deleteItem` will reference the correct thing. Now we have just one more thing to do before we can declare victory in deleting items. Open `TodoList.css` and make the following highlighted change and style rule addition:

```
.todoListMain .theList li {
  color: #333;
  background-color: rgba(255,255,255,.5);
  padding: 15px;
  margin-bottom: 15px;
  border-radius: 5px;

  transition: background-color .2s ease-out;
}


.todoListMain .theList li:hover {
  background-color: pink;
  cursor: pointer;
}
```

This provides the hover effect when you move the mouse cursor over the item that you want to remove. With this change done, our functionality to remove an item should be complete. Preview your app now and try adding some items and removing them. It should work well. And now on to just one more thing....

Animation! Animation! Animation!

Our very last task is to add some animations, to make adding and removing items look more natural. React offers many ways to animate something. You can use traditional approaches such as CSS animations, CSS transitions, `requestAnimationFrame`, the Web Animations API, or even a popular animation library. All of these approaches will take you far...very far.

When it comes to animating the existence of an element, though, the traditional approaches we outlined run into some limitations. This is because React entirely handles the lifecycle of an element as it is about to be deleted from the DOM. We can definitely override some of the lifecycle methods to intercept an element deletion and interject our own animation logic, but that gets us a bit too far into the weeds. We don't want to deal with that right now.

Fortunately, the React community has come up with a handful of lightweight animation libraries that make animating adding and deleting elements really easy. One such library is **Flip Move**. Among many things, this library makes animating the addition and removal of list elements simple.

To use this library, we need to first add it to our project. From the command line, make sure you are still in the same location as our todolist project and run the following command:

```
npm i -S react-flip-move
```

Click Enter/Return to copy all the necessary things locally into our project's `node_modules` folder. That's all the setup required. After you've done this, in `TodoItems.js`, add the following `import` statement at the top:

```
import FlipMove from 'react-flip-move';
```

Now all that's left is to tell our `FlipMove` component to animate our list of items. In our `render` function, make the following highlighted change:

```
render() {
  var todoEntries = this.props.entries;
  var listItems = todoEntries.map(this.createTasks);

  return (
    <ul className="theList">
      <FlipMove duration={250} easing="ease-out">
        {listItems}
      </FlipMove>
    </ul>
  );
}
```

We're simply wrapping our `listItems` (just before getting them printed) inside a `FlipMove` component and specifying the animation duration and the type of easing function to use. That's it. If you preview your app now, you'll see that adding and removing items doesn't just suddenly happen; these items are smoothly animated instead.

Uncontrolled Components vs. Controlled Components

Form elements are interesting. These are elements that contain some state on their own. For example, your `text` element might have some content in it, or you might have some items already selected in a drop-down list. React is all about centralizing state into its own little world, so it doesn't like that form elements have their own internal mechanism for storing state. The guidance is to synchronize all the form data inside a React component by using events such as `onChange`. These components that let React deal with form elements are known as **controlled components**.

Still, it's a hassle to have every form element deal with keeping state in sync. The React developers get that as well. The workaround is to do nothing. We simply let form elements deal with their own state and use refs to access the values when needed. That's what we did in this example. When we have components that defer all state management to the form DOM element, these components are known as **uncontrolled components**.

Conclusion

Our Todo app is pretty simple in what it does, but by building it from scratch, we covered almost every little interesting detail React brings to the table. More important, we created an example that shows how the various concepts we learned individually play together. That's truly actually the important detail.

Now here's a quick question for you: Does everything we've done in this chapter make sense? If so, you're in good shape to tell your friends and family that you're close to mastering React. If you still find some areas confusing, I recommend that you go back and reread the chapters that address your shortcomings.

Note: If you run into any issues, ask!

If you have any questions or your code isn't running like you expect, don't hesitate to ask! Post on the forums at https://forum.kirupa.com and get help from some of the friendliest and most knowledgeable people the Internet has ever brought together!

16

Creating a Sliding Menu in React

Sliding menus are all the rage in UIs today. All the cool kids are building them, and your friends probably just can't get enough of them. These menus are basically off-screen elements that slide into view when you click or tap on something. That *something* could be an arrow, a hamburger icon, or something else that indicates a menu will appear.

To see a sliding menu in action, go here: https://www.kirupa.com/react/examples/ slidingmenu_css/index.html.

You'll see a yellow menu with some navigation links smoothly slide in. If you click a navigation link or anywhere in the yellow region inside that menu, the menu slides back (really smoothly again, of course) and the content behind it reappears. Let's look at how to create all of this using React.

> **Note: For a Non-React Solution**
>
> If you're looking to create this menu using plain JavaScript without any React wizardry, the tutorial *Creating a Smooth Sliding Menu* (http://bit.ly/plainSidingMenu) has you covered.

How the Sliding Menu Works

Before we jump into the code, let's take a few moments to better understand how exactly our sliding menu works. Starting at the very top, we have our page that displays some content:

What you see initially!

When you decide to bring up the menu (by clicking/tapping the blue circle in our example), the menu magically slides into view:

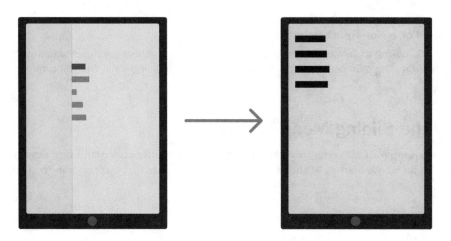

The way this sliding menu works isn't as crazy as it seems. The menu is never truly nonexistent; it is simply hidden outside the view. To see what that looks like, check out the following diagram:

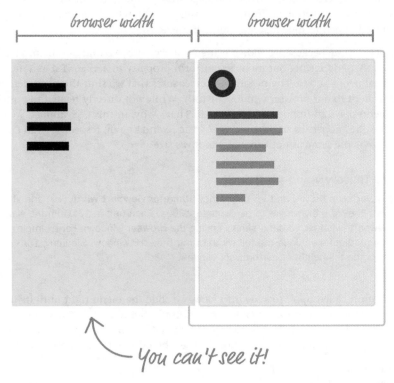

Just to the left of the content what we see is our menu, patiently hiding until it is called upon. We do that by shifting the menu as far left as we can until it's fully out of view. Figuring out how far to shift is easy. Our menu's size is the same as our browser's window (a.k.a. the viewport) size because we want the menu to fully cover up whatever is shown. Given that detail, we just shift the menu left by the browser's width. One way of doing that might be by using some CSS that looks as follows:

```
#theMenu {
  position: fixed;
  left: 0;
  top: 0;
  transform: translate3d(-100vw, 0, 0);

  width: 100vw;
  height: 100vh;
}
```

We set our menu's position to `fixed`. This single change gives our menu a whole lot of magical capabilities. For starters, it ensures that normal layout rules no longer apply to it. We can position our menu anywhere we want using normal x and y values, and the menu won't shift away from where we have it positioned. If that isn't awesome enough, our menu won't even display a scrollbar if we happen to hide it somewhere offscreen.

All this is a good thing because we hide our menu offscreen by setting our menu's left and top properties to 0 and setting our menu's transform property to a `translate3d` method with a horizontal value of `-100vw`. The negative value ensures that we shift the menu left by the amount equivalent to our browser window's width. While not directly related to position, the size of our menu plays an important role as well. That's why, in this CSS snippet, we have the `width` and `height` properties set with values of `100vw` and `100vh`, respectively, to ensure that our menu's size is the same as our browser window's size.

What Are These **vw** and **vh** Units?

If you've never seen the `vw` and `vh` units, they stand for **viewport width** (`vw`) and **viewport height** (`vh`). They're a bit similar to percentage values. Each unit is 1/100th the width or height of your viewport (what we've been simply calling the browser window). For example, a value of `100vw` means that its value is the full width of our browser window. Similarly, `100vh` refers to a value that is the full height of our browser window.

When the menu is called upon to slide into view, we slide the menu right until its horizontal position is the same as our browser window origin. If we had to look at what the CSS for it might look like, this would be an easy change from what we already have. We simply set our `transform` property's `translate3d` method and set the horizontal position to a value of `0vw`.

That might look something like this:

```
transform: translate3d(0vw, 0, 0);
```

This change ensures that our menu is shifted right from being hidden offscreen (with a horizontal translate value of `-100vw`) and is now visible. When our menu needs to disappear, we can translate it back:

```
transform: translate3d(-100vw, 0, 0);
```

The biggest thing we haven't spoken about is the animation that makes the sliding look cool. This is done using a simple CSS transition that animates the `transform` property:

```
transition: transform .3s cubic-bezier(0, .52, 0, 1);
```

If you're not familiar with CSS transitions, it's a very simple concept to wrap your brain around. I don't explain it here, so take a few moments and read through the short *Introduction to CSS Transitions* article (https://www.kirupa.com/html5/introduction_css_transitions.htm) for an overview.

So far, we've taken a bird's-eye view of how our sliding menu works. A few details need to be looked at, but we'll do that in the next couple sections when we actually build this menu.

Setting Up the Sliding Menu

Now that you have a basic idea about how a sliding menu works, let's turn all that theoretical knowledge into some sweet JSX and code. The first thing we're going to do is look at our example in terms of the individual components that will make it up.

At the very top, we have our `MenuContainer` component:

This component is responsible for doing nonvisual things like managing state, hosting our `Menu` and `MenuButton` components, and displaying some of the initial text. The bird's-eye view looks a bit like this:

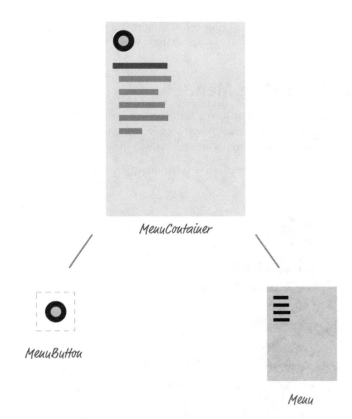

In the next few sections, we'll start creating these components and getting the example up and running.

Getting Started

Use `create-react-app` to create a new project called `slidingmenu`. If you aren't familiar with how to do that, check out Chapter 13, "Setting Up Your React Dev Environment Easily," to walk through the details of creating and working with React projects. After you've created your project, you want to start from a blank slate. Delete everything in your `public` and `src` folders. You'll re-create the necessary pieces shortly.

Let's start by creating our HTML document. In your `public` folder, create a file called `index.html`. Inside it, add the following contents:

```
<!DOCTYPE html>
<html>

<head>
  <title>Sliding Menu in React</title>
</head>
```

```
<body>
  <div id="container"></div>
</body>

</html>
```

This HTML page is simply the destination where all of our React components will eventually render their output.

Next, you want to create a file called `index.js` in the `src` folder that will be responsible for teeing things up in the code. Add the following content into this file:

```
import React from "react";
import ReactDOM from "react-dom";
import "./index.css";
import MenuContainer from "./MenuContainer";

ReactDOM.render(
  <MenuContainer/>,
  document.querySelector("#container")
);
```

The `render` call here is responsible for displaying the output of our `MenuContainer` component into the `container` `div` element we specified in HTML a few moments ago. In our `import` statements, besides pulling in the `react` and `react-dom` libraries, we are referencing `index.css` and our `MenuContainer` component. That's all there is to our `index.js` file.

Next we're going to create the `index.css` file in our `src` folder and get the page's basic styling defined. In this file, add the following two style rules:

```
body {
  background-color: #EEE;
  font-family: sans-serif;
  font-size: 20px;
  padding: 25px;
  margin: 0;
  overflow: auto;
}

#container li {
  margin-bottom: 10px;
}
```

There isn't much to say about these style rules, so the last thing we do to get our initial app set up is create our `MenuContainer` component. Create a file called `MenuContainer.js` in the `src` folder and add the following JS and JSX into it:

```
import React, { Component } from "react";

class MenuContainer extends Component {
  render() {
    return (
```

```
      <div>
        <div>
          <p>Can you spot the item that doesn't belong?</p>
          <ul>
            <li>Lorem</li>
            <li>Ipsum</li>
            <li>Dolor</li>
            <li>Sit</li>
            <li>Bumblebees</li>
            <li>Aenean</li>
            <li>Consectetur</li>
          </ul>
        </div>
      </div>
    );
  }
}

export default MenuContainer;
```

Be sure to save the changes you made to all of your files, and test your app (using `npm start`) to ensure that your initial setup of the app works fine. If everything worked out properly, your default browser will launch and you'll see something that looks as follows:

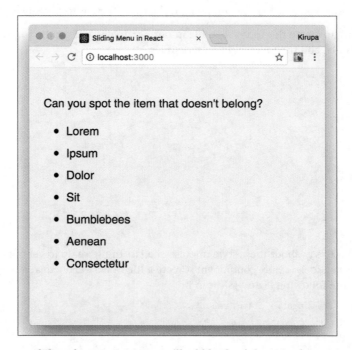

There's no menu to slide or button to press; we'll add both of those in the next couple sections.

Showing and Hiding the Menu

With the initial setup out of the way, it's time for the fun part: actually building the menu. Our menu is shown or hidden as follows:

1. When you click a button, the menu slides into view.

2. When you click anywhere on the menu, the menu slides out of view.

This means that we need to account for a few things going on. We need to maintain some state to keep track of whether the menu is hidden or shown. This state needs to be something we update from both the button and the menu because clicking on either will toggle whether the menu is visible. We need our state to live in a common location that both the menu and the button can access. That common location will be inside our `MenuContainer` component, so let's add the code relating to our state logic.

In the `MenuContainer.js` file, add the constructor and `toggleMenu` methods just above our `render` method:

```
constructor(props) {
  super(props);

  this.state = {
    visible: false
  };

  this.toggleMenu = this.toggleMenu.bind(this);
}

toggleMenu() {
  this.setState({
    visible: !this.state.visible
  });
}
```

The code you've just added should look like a walk in the park by now. You're storing a variable called `visible` in your state object, and you're creating a method called `toggleMenu` that will be responsible for toggling whether `visible` is `true` or `false`.

Next up is dealing with the `click` events on the button and menu. If the goal is to update our state from inside our `MenuContainer` component, we need to place our event handler inside `MenuContainer` as well. Go ahead and add the following highlighted lines:

```
import React, { Component } from "react";

class MenuContainer extends Component {
  constructor(props) {
    super(props);

    this.state = {
      visible: false
    };
```

```
    this.handleMouseDown = this.handleMouseDown.bind(this);
    this.toggleMenu = this.toggleMenu.bind(this);
  }

  handleMouseDown(e) {
    this.toggleMenu();

    console.log("clicked");
    e.stopPropagation();
  }

  toggleMenu() {
    this.setState({
      visible: !this.state.visible
    });
  }
  .
  .
  .
}
```

When the handleMouseDown method is called, we call toggleMenu, which toggles whether the menu appears. At this point, you're probably wondering where the actual code for dealing with a click event is. What exactly will trigger a call to handleMouseDown? The answer is, nothing so far! We've done things in a bit of a reverse order and defined our event handler first. We handle the association between our event handler and our click event in a few moments when dealing with our button and menu components.

Creating the Button

In your src folder, create two files called MenuButton.js and MenuButton.css. Then open MenuButton.js in your code editor. Inside it, add the following lines of code:

```
import React, { Component } from "react";
import './MenuButton.css';

class MenuButton extends Component {
  render() {
    return (
      <button id="roundButton"
              onMouseDown={this.props.handleMouseDown}></button>
    );
  }
}

export default MenuButton;
```

Take a moment to see what this code is doing. There isn't a whole lot going on. We define a button element called roundButton, and we associate the onMouseDown event with a prop we are referencing as `handleMouseDown`. Before moving on, open `MenuButton.css` and add the following style rules:

```css
#roundButton {
  background-color: #96D9FF;
  margin-bottom: 20px;
  width: 50px;
  height: 50px;
  border-radius: 50%;
  border: 10px solid #0065A6;
  outline: none;
  transition: all .2s cubic-bezier(0, 1.26, .8, 1.28);
}

#roundButton:hover {
  background-color: #96D9FF;
  cursor: pointer;
  border-color: #003557;
  transform: scale(1.2, 1.2);
}

#roundButton:active {
  border-color: #003557;
  background-color: #FFF;
}
```

Now it's is time to actually instantiate our newly created `MenuButton` component. Go back to the `MenuContainer` component and add the following highlighted line inside the `render` method:

```jsx
render() {
  return (
    <MenuButton handleMouseDown={this.handleMouseDown}/>
      .
      .
      .
  );
}
```

For this line to actually do something, be sure to add the appropriate `import` statement at the top for our `MenuButton.js` file. That's an easy one to overlook!

Notice that we are passing in a prop called `handleMouseDown`, and its value is the `handle-MouseDown` event handler that we defined earlier. This ensures that when you click the button inside the `MenuButton` component, the `handleMouseDown` method that lives in the `MenuContainer` component gets called. All of this is great, but our button isn't very useful without a menu to help slide into view. We'll fix that next.

Creating the Menu

It's time to create our `Menu` component that will be responsible for all things dealing with the menu. Before we actually create this component, let's pretend that it already exists and call it from our `render` method inside our `MenuContainer`. Add the following highlighted call to our (currently imaginary) `Menu` component just below where you added the call to `MenuButton` a few short moments earlier:

```
render() {
  return (
    <MenuButton handleMouseDown={this.handleMouseDown} />
    <Menu handleMouseDown={this.handleMouseDown}
          menuVisibility={this.state.visible} />

      .
      .
      .

  );
}
```

Add the import statement for `Menu.js` as well. Getting back to the `Menu` component, look at the props you're passing in. The first prop should look familiar to you. It is `handleMouseDown` and its value is our `handleMouseDown` event-handling method. The second prop is called `menuVisibility`. Its value is the current value of our `visible` state property. Now let's go ahead and actually create our `Menu` component and see, among other things, how these props get used.

In the same `src` folder we have been partying in for the past few sections, add one file called `Menu.js` and another file called `Menu.css`. Inside `Menu.js`, add the following contents:

```
import React, { Component } from "react";
import "./Menu.css";

class Menu extends Component {
  render() {
    var visibility = "hide";

    if (this.props.menuVisibility) {
      visibility = "show";
    }

    return (
      <div id="flyoutMenu"
           onMouseDown={this.props.handleMouseDown}
           className={visibility}>
        <h2><a href="#">Home</a></h2>
        <h2><a href="#">About</a></h2>
        <h2><a href="#">Contact</a></h2>
        <h2><a href="#">Search</a></h2>
      </div>
    );
  }
}

export default Menu;
```

Pay attention to the JSX in the `return` statement. We have a `div` element called `flyoutMenu` with some sample content. In our `div` element, we call our `handleMouseDown` event-handling method (passed in via a prop) when the `onMouseDown` event is overheard. Next, we set a `class` value on this element; the value is the result of evaluating a variable called `visibility`. As you might recall, `class` is a reserved name in JavaScript and you can't use it directly in our JSX; it has to be specified as `className`.

Getting back to our code, the value of `visibility` is set a few lines earlier:

```
var visibility = "hide";

if (this.props.menuVisibility) {
  visibility = "show";
}
```

The value is either `hide` or `show`, depending on whether the `menuVisibility` prop (whose value is specified by our `visible` state property) is `true` or `false`. While it might not look like it, the code revolving around `className` plays a really important role in determining whether your menu is actually visible. When we look at our CSS, you'll see why. Now open `Menu.css` and add the following style rules into it:

```css
#flyoutMenu {
  width: 100vw;
  height: 100vh;
  background-color: #FFE600;
  position: fixed;
  top: 0;
  left: 0;
  transition: transform .3s
              cubic-bezier(0, .52, 0, 1);
  overflow: scroll;
  z-index: 1000;
}

#flyoutMenu.hide {
  transform: translate3d(-100vw, 0, 0);
}

#flyoutMenu.show {
  transform: translate3d(0vw, 0, 0);
  overflow: hidden;
}

#flyoutMenu h2 a {
  color: #333;
  margin-left: 15px;
  text-decoration: none;
}
```

```
#flyoutMenu h2 a:hover {
  text-decoration: underline;
}
```

The CSS you see here mostly deals with how our menu itself looks, but the actual showing and hiding of the menu is handled by the `#flyoutMenu.hide` and `#flyoutMenu.show` style rules. Which of these style rules becomes active depends entirely on the code we looked at earlier. In our `flyoutMenu div` element, remember that the `class` value on the generated HTML (which our CSS maps to) will be either `hide` or `show`, depending on what value we set for `className`. Pretty cool, right?

At this point, we're fully done with all our coding. Be sure to save all your changes and ensure that the app works just like the example we started with. Don't nuke this project, though. We'll be revisiting this and addressing some major shortcomings in a little bit.

Conclusion

This is one of the first examples we've looked at in which we're using React to create a common UI occurrence, a sliding menu. As part of this, you learned more about the interplay between components, such as dealing with events/event handlers, sharing state, and so on. As we look at more examples together, you'll see that there isn't a whole lot more to React than what you've seen here. All that remains is a clever arrangement and rearrangement of the same concepts in more complex scenarios. This doesn't mean we're done, though. There's more React to be had and more examples to create and fully understand!

Note: If you run into any issues, ask!

If you have any questions or your code isn't running like you expect, don't hesitate to ask! Post on the forums at https://forum.kirupa.com and get help from some of the friendliest and most knowledgeable people the Internet has ever brought together!

17

Avoiding Unnecessary Renders in React

You're probably really tired of me saying this, but fast DOM performance is one of the biggest feathers in React's cap. That doesn't mean you get all that great performance for free, though. While React handles a lot of the heavy lifting, you should consciously take certain steps to ensure that your app isn't doing unnecessary work and slowing things down. One of the biggest steps involves making sure each component's `render` method is called only when it absolutely has to be. In the next few sections, we'll look at why that's a problem and what you can do about it.

About the `render` Method

The `render` method's official job description is pretty simple. It just needs to show up on each component and help generate the JSX to return to whatever parent component called it. If we had to loosely describe the full workflow from components on one end and a fully finished app on the other end, it would look as follows:

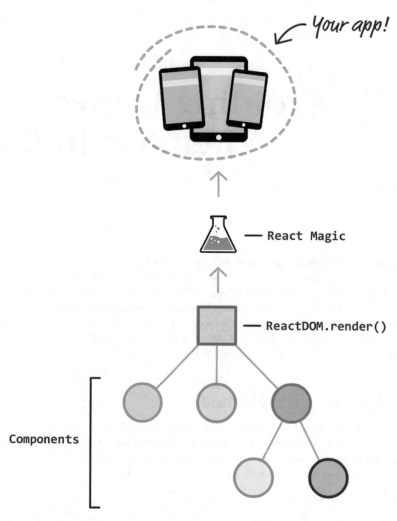

You have your finished app on one side. You have the components that make up the app on the other. Inside all these components, you see render methods returning bits and chunks of JSX getting combined with more bits and chunks of JSX from other components. This process repeats until you get the final JSX at the root of the component hierarchy where we have our ReactDOM.render call. From there, the **React Magic** happens that turns all this JSX into the appropriate HTML/CSS/JS to display in the browser.

Now that you have a very basic idea of how React works, let's get back into the weeds where our components and their render methods live. In all the React code you've written so far, you might also have noticed that you never had to explicitly call the render method on any component. That just sort of happened automatically. Let's get more precise here. Three things cause a `render` method to automatically get called:

1. A prop that lives on your component gets updated.

2. A state property that lives on your component gets updated.

3. A parent component's `render` method gets called.

All three of these cases seem like good examples of when we want our component's `render` method to be automatically called. After all, all three of these cases *could* cause your visual state to change, right?

The answer is, well, *it depends!* Very often, components find themselves being forced to re-render even though the prop or state that is changing has absolutely nothing to do with them. In some situations, a parent component is correctly rendering or re-rendering, but that is localized to just that component. There's no need to ask the child components to re-render for something that doesn't affect them.

Now, I might be painting an alarming picture of unnecessary work that has been going on right under our noses. One point to keep in mind is that a `render` method being called is not the same thing as the DOM ultimately getting updated. React takes a few additional steps in which the DOM is diffed (that is, the previous version is compared with the new/current version) to truly see if any changes need to be represented. All of these "few additional steps" means work, and more complex apps with a lot of components will face many instances that will start to add up. Some of this is additional work done by React's internals. Some of it are just important things we do in our `render` methods; we often have a lot of code there to help generate the appropriate JSX. Rarely does our `render` method return a static piece of JSX with no evaluation or calculation happening, so minimizing unnecessary `render` calls is a good thing.

Optimizing render Calls

Now that we've looked at the problem, let's examine some approaches we can use to ensure that we're calling a component's `render` method only when absolutely necessary. The following sections walk you through this.

Getting an Example Going

To help make sense of this, we're going to look at an example. It's not just any example, either. We'll revisit our sliding menu that we created earlier. If you have it handy, go ahead and open it in your code editor.

If you don't have the project handy, that's okay. Use `create-react-app` to create a new React project and overwrite everything in your `src` and `public` folders with the contents from the Sliding Menu Github repo:

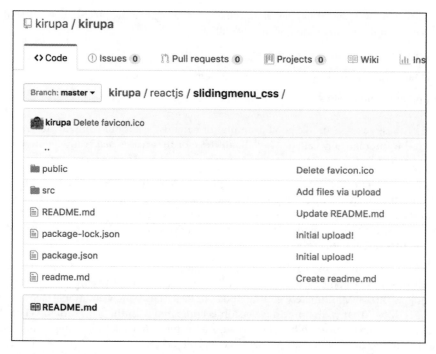

When you have the sliding menu project ready, run it in your browser to make sure that everything works—or still works.

If you haven't completed the sliding menu from the previous chapter, I highly encourage you to do so. Having the working project handy is all fine and good, but knowing how the code works and understanding some of the choices we made during implementation is important. You can certainly follow along without understanding that chapter, but don't say I didn't warn you if some of the code you're about to see seems a bit out of place.

Looking at our example, to reuse a graphic you've already seen, the component hierarchy for our sliding menu app looks as follows:

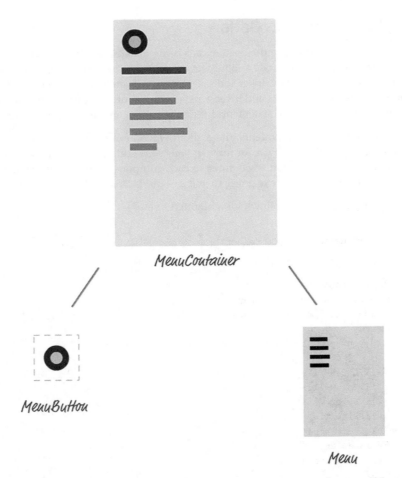

MenuContainer

MenuButton

Menu

At the root is MenuContainer, and it has two children: MenuButton and Menu. Although it's not shown in the diagram, there's a ReactDOM.render call in index.js that exposes our MenuContainer to the DOM:

```
ReactDOM.render(
  <MenuContainer/>,
  document.getElementById("container")
);
```

When the button rendered by MenuButton is clicked, we set a Boolean state property (called visible) in MenuContainer to true. This state property change triggers our Menu component to update a class value that activates the appropriate CSS to slide our menu in. Clicking anywhere in the menu dismisses the menu by undoing what was done via setting the state property in MenuContainer to false.

Seeing the `render` Calls

The first thing we want to do is see the `render` calls being made. You can do this in many ways. You can set a break point in your code and inspect the results using your browser's developer tools. You can install the React Developer Tools add-on (for Chrome or Firefox) from https://github.com/facebook/react-devtools and inspect each component. You can also take a very simple approach and insert `console.log` statements inside the `render` methods you're interested in.

Because we have only three components in our sliding menu example, the `console.log` approach is an easy one that we'll use for now. In your code editor, open `MenuContainer.js`, `MenuButton.js`, and `Menu.js` and scroll down to each component's respective `render` method. At the very top of this method, we're going to add a `console.log` call.

In `MenuContainer.js`, add the following highlighted line:

```
render() {
  console.log("Rendering: MenuContainer");
  return (
    <div>
      <MenuButton handleMouseDown={this.handleMouseDown}/>
      <Menu handleMouseDown={this.handleMouseDown}
            menuVisibility={this.state.visible}/>
      <div>
        <p>Can you spot the item that doesn&apos;t belong?</p>
        <ul>
          <li>Lorem</li>
          <li>Ipsum</li>
          <li>Dolor</li>
          <li>Sit</li>
          <li>Bumblebees</li>
          <li>Aenean</li>
          <li>Consectetur</li>
        </ul>
      </div>
    </div>
  );
}
```

Let's do something similar in `MenuButton.js`:

```
render() {
  console.log("Rendering: MenuButton");

  return (
    <button id="roundButton"
            onMouseDown={this.props.handleMouseDown}></button>
  );
}
```

Lastly, add the following highlighted line in `Menu.js`:

```
render() {
  console.log("Rendering: Menu");
```

```
var visibility = "hide";

if (this.props.menuVisibility) {
  visibility = "show";
}

return (
  <div id="flyoutMenu"
       onMouseDown={this.props.handleMouseDown}
       className={visibility}>
    <h2><a href="#">Home</a></h2>
    <h2><a href="#">About</a></h2>
    <h2><a href="#">Contact</a></h2>
    <h2><a href="#">Search</a></h2>
  </div>
);
}
```

Once you have added these three lines, run your app in your browser. Once the app is up and running, bring up your browser's developer tools and take a look at what is printed in the console:

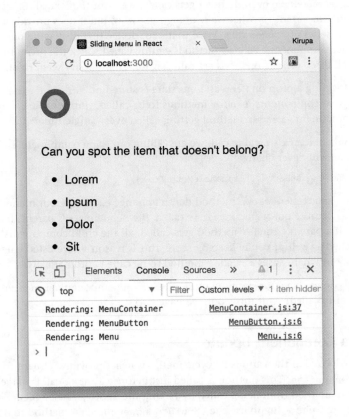

You might see warnings and other stuff displayed, but look for the output of the `console.log` statements you added. When you first run your app, you'll see that all three of our components have their respective `render` method getting called. This is expected because it's the first time your app is being loaded.

With your console still open, go ahead and click the blue button to bring up the menu. Then take a look at your console. You'll see the following new items (highlighted in green):

Rendering: MenuContainer

Rendering: MenuButton

Rendering: Menu

clicked

Rendering: MenuContainer

Rendering: MenuButton

Rendering: Menu

When the `handleMouseDown` event handler gets called, we print the text `clicked` to the console. This isn't important for what we're doing right now, but it does provide a nice separation between our series of `render` calls. With that said, notice that displaying our menu results in all three of our components' `render` methods getting called. Click the menu to dismiss it. You'll see that all three `render` methods get called again. That doesn't seem right, does it?

Because we're toggling a prop on `Menu` and our state is stored on `MenuContainer`, it makes sense for those two components' `render` methods to be called...for now. But, why is our `MenuButton` component's `render` method getting called every single time?

Looking at `MenuContainer`'s `render` call, we are calling our `Menu` component and passing in a prop whose value will never change:

```
<MenuButton handleMouseDown={this.handleMouseDown}/>
```

The value of our `handleMouseDown` method doesn't change each time our menu is opened or closed. This is because our `MenuContainer` (a.k.a. the `MenuButton`'s parent) has its `render` method called. If a parent's `render` method gets called, all the child components' `render` methods get called as well. If you're keeping score, this is reason #3 we listed a few sections ago when talking about what causes a `render` method to be called automatically.

So what options do we have for stopping our `MenuButton` component's `render` method from being unnecessarily called? As it turns out, we have two.

Overriding a Component Update

A while ago, we looked at the various lifecycle methods React provides. One of them is `shouldComponentUpdate`. This method is called just before a `render` call is made, and you can block the `render` method from being called by having the `shouldComponentUpdate` method return `false`. Here we're going to use the `shouldComponentUpdate` method to do just that.

Inside the `MenuButton` component, add the following highlighted lines:

```
import React, { Component } from "react";
import "./MenuButton.css";

class MenuButton extends Component {
  shouldComponentUpdate(nextProps, nextState) {
    return false;
  }

  render() {
    console.log("Rendering: MenuButton");

    return (
      <button id="roundButton"
              onMouseDown={this.props.handleMouseDown}></button>
    );
  }
}

export default MenuButton;
```

Refresh your app to test your code. Pay attention to the console and see what gets printed when you're showing and hiding a menu. Your output when your page loads and the menu is displayed for the first time now appears as follows:

Rendering: MenuContainer

Rendering: MenuButton

Rendering: Menu

clicked

Rendering: MenuContainer

Rendering: Menu

Notice that our `MenuButton` component's `render` method isn't called. That's great. Before we celebrate too much, though, we've really taken a hammer to our problem by always returning `false` when `shouldComponentUpdate` gets called. While that works for what we are doing, let's be a bit more careful to ensure that we aren't accidentally preventing valid updates in the future if we eventually modify `MenuButton` and how it gets used.

When you look at the `shouldComponentUpdate` method's signature, you can see that two arguments are passed in. One is for the next `prop` value, and the other is for the next `state` value. We can use these arguments to compare the present with the future and act a bit more intelligently about whether we allow our `render` call to be made. In the case of `MenuButton`, the only prop we're passing in is for the value of `handleMouseDown`. We can check to ensure that this value doesn't change by modifying the `shouldComponentUpdate` method, as follows:

```
shouldComponentUpdate(nextProps, nextState) {
  if (nextProps.handleMouseDown === this.props.handleMouseDown) {
    return false;
  } else {
    return true;
  }
}
```

This code ensures that we don't unnecessarily call `render` if the value of `handleMouseDown` stays the same. If the value of `handleMouseDown` changed, we could properly return a value of `true` to allow the `render` call to be made. You can use other criteria to specify whether the component's `render` method should get called, and what you do depends entirely on the component in question. Feel free to get creative, if you need to.

Using `PureComponent`

It's a common occurrence to have components forced to re-render despite not having relevant prop or state changes. Our `MenuButton` example is just one such occurrence. The solution is to call `shouldComponentUpdate` and check whether any prop or state changes have taken place. To avoid having to make this check all the time, a special kind of component can handle this checking automatically for you. That component is `PureComponent`.

Until now, all of our components have been based on `Component`:

```
class Blah extends Component {
  render() {
    return (
      <h1>Hello!</h1>
    );
  }
}
```

To base our components off `PureComponent`, all you have to do is this:

```
class Blah extends PureComponent {
  render() {
    return (
      <h1>Hello!</h1>
    );
  }
}
```

That's pretty much it. Your component will now be extra careful about calling `render` only when it determines that a change to either the prop or state has actually been made. To see this for yourself, you can change `MenuButton` to be a `PureComponent` instead of just a `Component`.

In `MenuButton.js`, first delete the `shouldComponentUpdate` method; you don't need it anymore. Then make the following two highlighted changes:

```
import React, { PureComponent } from "react";
import "./MenuButton.css";

class MenuButton extends PureComponent {
  render() {
    console.log("Rendering: MenuButton");

    return (
      <button id="roundButton"
              onMouseDown={this.props.handleMouseDown}></button>
    );
  }
}

export default MenuButton;
```

We first import the necessary code from the React library to make `PureComponent` work. Next, we extend our `MenuButton` from `PureComponent`. That's it. If you test your app now and inspect the console after displaying the menu, you'll see that our `MenuButton` component's `render` method doesn't get called when your menu decides to show up (or disappear).

Why Not Always Use `PureComponent`?

The `PureComponent` seems pretty awesome, right? Why don't we just use it always and ditch `Component` altogether? We probably should! With that said, there are a few reasons you might want to stick with `Component`.

First, `PureComponent` performs what's known as a shallow comparison. It isn't a comprehensive check of everything that might have changed in your props or state between calls to re-render. For many cases, that's okay. For other cases, that might not be. Keep that in mind when using `PureComponent`. You might find that you need to write your own `shouldComponentUpdate` and handle the updating logic manually. You can't use `PureComponent` and specify `shouldComponentUpdate` at the same time, although that makes a nice try!

Beyond the comparison logic, the bigger problem with using `PureComponent` is performance. Having each of your components check to see if props or state have changed, even if it's a shallow check, takes up computation time. Remember, these checks happen every time your component decides to re-render or is asked to re-render by a parent. For complex UIs, that could happen frequently without you even realizing it.

TL;DR: This should probably have been mentioned at the top of this note, but what are you going to do? Basically, it's fine to use `PureComponent` instead of `Component`. Just be aware of the two (minor) side effects.

Conclusion

Ensuring that your app is performant requires constant vigilance. Profile your app's performance frequently, and definitely do so each time you make a code change with the goal of optimizing performance. Each performance optimization you make brings complexity that just adds to your (or your team's) overhead of maintaining the code and making fixes in it for the lifetime of your app. Be conscious and don't overoptimize. If your app works really well on the devices and browsers you're targeting (especially the low-end ones), consider your job done. Take a break and don't do any extra work!

> **Note: If you run into any issues, ask!**
>
> If you have any questions or your code isn't running like you expect, don't hesitate to ask! Post on the forums at https://forum.kirupa.com and get help from some of the friendliest and most knowledgeable people the Internet has ever brought together!

18

Creating a Single-Page App in React Using React Router

Now that you've familiarized yourself with the basics of how to work with React, let's kick things up a few notches. Here we're going to use React to build a simple **single-page app** (also referred to as **SPA** by the cool kids and people living in Scandinavia). As we talked about in our React introduction forever ago, single-page apps are different from the more traditional multipage apps that you see everywhere. The biggest difference is that navigating a single-page app doesn't involve going to an entirely new page. Instead, your pages (commonly known as *views* in this context) typically load inline within the same page itself:

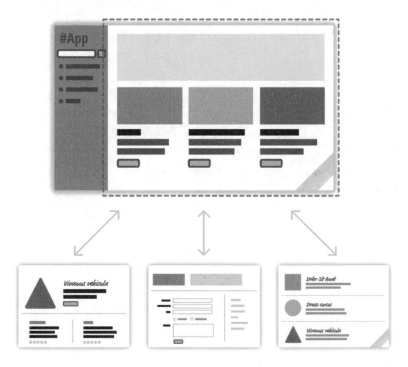

When you're loading content inline, things get a little challenging. The hard part isn't loading the content itself. That's relatively easy. The hard part is making sure that single-page apps behave in a way that is consistent with what your users are accustomed to. More specifically, when users navigate your app, they have some expectations:

1. The URL displayed in the address bar should always reflect the thing users are viewing.

2. Users expect to be able to use the browser's back and forward buttons successfully.

3. Users should be able to navigate to a particular view (a.k.a. **deep link**) directly using the appropriate URL.

With multipage apps, these three things come for free. You don't have to do anything extra for any of it. With single-page apps, because you aren't navigating to an entirely new page, you have to do real work to deal with these three things *that your users expect to just work*. You need to ensure that navigating within your app adjusts the URL appropriately. You need to ensure that your browser's history is properly synchronized with each navigation to allow users to use the back and forward buttons. If users bookmark a particular view or copy/paste a URL to access later, you need to ensure that your single-page app takes them to the correct place.

To deal with all of this, you have a bucket full of techniques commonly known as **routing**. With routing, you try to map URLs to destinations that aren't physical pages, such as the individual views in your single-page app. That sounds complicated, but fortunately, a bunch of JavaScript libraries can help with this. One such JavaScript library is the star of this tutorial, React Router(https://github.com/reactjs/react-router). React Router provides routing capabilities to single-page apps built in React. What makes it nice is that it extends what you already know about React in familiar ways to give you all of this routing awesomeness. In this tutorial, you'll learn all about how it does that...and hopefully more.

Onward!

The Example

Before we go further, take a look at the following example in your browser: https://www.kirupa .com/react/examples/react_router/index.html.

Here, you have a simple React app that uses React Router to provide all the navigation and view-loading goodness:

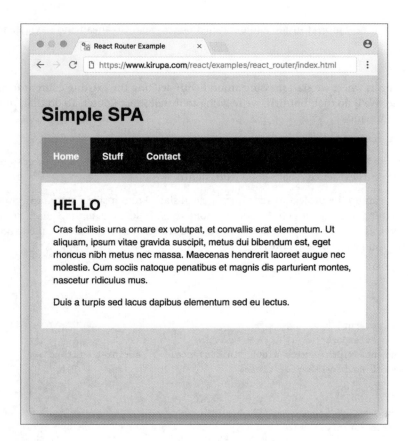

Click the various links to load the relevant content, and feel free to open this page in its own browser window (https://www.kirupa.com/react/examples/react_router/index.html) to use the back and forward buttons and see them working.

In the following sections, we're going to be building this app in pieces. By the end, not only will you have re-created this app, but hopefully you'll have learned enough about React Router to build cooler and even more awesome things.

Getting Started

First we need to get our project set up. We'll use our trusty `create-react-app` command to do this. From your favorite terminal, navigate to the folder where you want to create your app and type the following:

```
create-react-app react_spa
```

This creates our new project inside a folder called `react_spa`. Go ahead and navigate into this folder:

```
cd react_spa
```

Normally, this is where we start messing around with deleting the existing content to start from a blank slate. We'll do that, but first, we're going to install React Router. To do that, run the following command:

```
npm i react-router-dom --save
```

This copies the appropriate React Router files and registers it in our `package.json` so that our app is aware of its existence. That's good stuff, right?

It's time to clean up the project to start from a clean slate. From inside your `react_spa` folder, delete everything inside your `public` and `src` folders. Now, let's create the `index.html` file that will serve as our app's starting point. In your `public` folder, create a file called `index.html` and add the following contents into it:

```
<!DOCTYPE html>
<html>

<head>
  <meta charset="utf-8">
  <meta name="viewport"
        content="width=device-width, initial-scale=1, shrink-to-fit=no">
  <title>React Router Example</title>
</head>

<body>
  <div id="root"></div>
</body>

</html>
```

Take a quick glance at the HTML. You shouldn't see anything surprising here. Next, we'll create our JavaScript entry point. Inside the `src` folder, create a file called `index.js` and add the following contents into it:

```
import React from "react";
import ReactDOM from "react-dom";
import Main from "./Main";

ReactDOM.render(
  <Main/>,
  document.getElementById("root")
);
```

Our `ReactDOM.render` call lives here, and we're rendering our `Main` component...which doesn't exist yet. The `Main` component will be the starting point for our SPA expedition using React Router, and you'll see how beginning with the next section.

Building Our Single-Page App

The way we build our app is no different than the way we've been building all the apps so far. We'll have a main parent component. Each individual "page" of our app will be a separate component that feeds into the main component. The magic React Router brings to the table is basically choosing which components to show and which to hide. To make this feel natural and seamless, all of this *navigating* is tied in with our browser's address bar and back/forward buttons.

Displaying the Initial Frame

When building an SPA, a part of your page will always remain static. This static part, also referred to as an ***app frame***, could be one invisible HTML element that acts as the container for all of your content, or it could include some additional visual things such as a header, a footer, or navigation. In our case, our app frame will be a component that contains UI elements for our navigation header and an empty area for content to load in.

Inside our `src` folder, create a new file called `Main.js` and add the following content into it:

```
import React, { Component } from "react";

class Main extends Component {
  render() {
    return (
      <div>
        <h1>Simple SPA</h1>
        <ul className="header">
          <li><a href="/">Home</a></li>
          <li><a href="/stuff">Stuff</a></li>
          <li><a href="/contact">Contact</a></li>
        </ul>
        <div className="content">

        </div>
      </div>
    );
  }
}

export default Main;
```

Take a look at what we have here. We have a component called `Main` that returns some HTML. That's it. To see what we have so far in action, type **npm start** and see what's going on in your browser.

You should see an unstyled version of an app title and some list items:

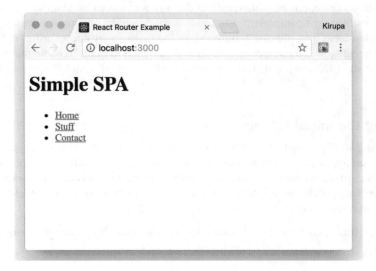

This doesn't look all fancy and styled, but that's okay for now; we'll deal with that later. The important thing to call out is that there's nothing React Router specific here—absolutely nothing!

Creating Our Content Pages

Our app will have three pages of content. This content will be just a simple component that prints out some JSX. Let's get that created and out of the way. First, create a file called `Home.js` in the `src` directory and add the following content:

```
import React, { Component } from "react";

class Home extends Component {
  render() {
    return (
      <div>
        <h2>HELLO</h2>
        <p>Cras facilisis urna ornare ex volutpat, et
        convallis erat elementum. Ut aliquam, ipsum vitae
        gravida suscipit, metus dui bibendum est, eget rhoncus nibh
        metus nec massa. Maecenas hendrerit laoreet augue
        nec molestie. Cum sociis natoque penatibus et magnis
        dis parturient montes, nascetur ridiculus mus.</p>

        <p>Duis a turpis sed lacus dapibus elementum sed eu lectus.</p>
      </div>
    );
  }
}

export default Home;
```

Next, create a file called `Stuff.js` in the same location and add in the following:

```
import React, { Component } from "react";

class Stuff extends Component {
  render() {
    return (
      <div>
        <h2>STUFF</h2>
        <p>Mauris sem velit, vehicula eget sodales vitae,
        rhoncus eget sapien:</p>
        <ol>
          <li>Nulla pulvinar diam</li>
          <li>Facilisis bibendum</li>
          <li>Vestibulum vulputate</li>
          <li>Eget erat</li>
          <li>Id porttitor</li>
        </ol>
      </div>
    );
  }
}

export default Stuff;
```

We have just one more page left. Create a file called `Contact.js` in the `src` folder and make sure its contents are the following:

```
import React, { Component } from "react";

class Contact extends Component {
  render() {
    return (
      <div>
        <h2>GOT QUESTIONS?</h2>
        <p>The easiest thing to do is post on
        our <a href="http://forum.kirupa.com">forums</a>.
        </p>
      </div>
    );
  }
}

export default Contact;
```

That's the last of the content we're going to add. If you take a look at what you're adding, you'll see that these components can't get any simpler. They just return some boilerplate JSX content. Be sure to save all your changes to these three files. We'll look at how to make them useful shortly.

Using React Router

We have our app frame in the form of our `Main` component. We have our content pages represented by the `Home`, `Stuff`, and `Contact` components. Now we need to tie all of these together to create our app. This is where React Router comes in. To start using it, go back to `Main.js` and ensure that your `import` statements look as follows:

```
import React, { Component } from "react";
import {
  Route,
  NavLink,
  HashRouter
} from "react-router-dom";
import Home from "./Home";
import Stuff from "./Stuff";
import Contact from "./Contact";
```

We are importing `Route`, `NavLink`, and `HashRouter` from the `react-router-dom` NPM package installed earlier. In addition, we're importing our `Home`, `Stuff`, and `Contact` components because we'll be referencing them as part of loading our content.

React Router works by defining what I call a **routing region**. Inside this region are two things:

1. Your navigation links

2. The container to load your content into

There's a close correlation between the URL your navigation links specify and the content that ultimately gets loaded. There's no way to easily explain this without first getting our hands dirty and implementing what you just read about.

The first thing to do is define the **routing region**. Inside our `Main` component's `render` method, add the following highlighted lines:

```
class Main extends Component {
  render() {
    return (
      <HashRouter>
        <div>
          <h1>Simple SPA</h1>
          <ul className="header">
            <li><a href="/">Home</a></li>
            <li><a href="/stuff">Stuff</a></li>
            <li><a href="/contact">Contact</a></li>
          </ul>
```

```
            <div className="content">

            </div>
          </div>
        </HashRouter>
      );
    }
}
```

The `HashRouter` component provides the foundation for the navigation and browser history handling that routing is made up of. Next we need to define our navigation links. We already have list elements with the `a` element defined. We need to replace them with the more specialized `NavLink` component, so go ahead and make the following highlighted changes:

```
class Main extends Component {
  render() {
    return (
      <HashRouter>
        <div>
          <h1>Simple SPA</h1>
          <ul className="header">
            <li><NavLink to="/">Home</NavLink></li>
            <li><NavLink to="/stuff">Stuff</NavLink></li>
            <li><NavLink to="/contact">Contact</NavLink></li>
          </ul>
          <div className="content">

          </div>
        </div>
      </HashRouter>
    );
  }
}
```

For each link, pay attention to the URL we're telling our router to navigate to. This URL value (defined by the `to` prop) acts as an identifier to ensure that the right content gets loaded. We match the URL with the content by using a `Route` component. Go ahead and add the following highlighted lines:

```
class Main extends Component {
  render() {
    return (
      <HashRouter>
        <div>
          <h1>Simple SPA</h1>
          <ul className="header">
            <li><NavLink to="/">Home</NavLink></li>
            <li><NavLink to="/stuff">Stuff</NavLink></li>
            <li><NavLink to="/contact">Contact</NavLink></li>
          </ul>
```

```
        <div className="content">
          <Route path="/" component={Home}/>
          <Route path="/stuff" component={Stuff}/>
          <Route path="/contact" component={Contact}/>
        </div>
      </div>
    </HashRouter>
  );
  }
}
```

As you can see, the `Route` component contains a path prop. The value you specify for the path determines when this route is going to be active. When a route is active, the component specified by the component prop gets rendered. For example, when we click on the `Stuff` link (whose path is `/stuff` as set by the NavLink component's to prop), the route whose path value is also `/stuff` becomes active. This means the contents of our `Stuff` component get rendered.

You can see all of this for yourself. Jump back to your browser to see the live updates or run `npm start` again. Click around on the links to see the content loading in and out. Something seems off, though, right? The content for our home page seems to always display even if we're clicking on the `Stuff` or `Contact` links:

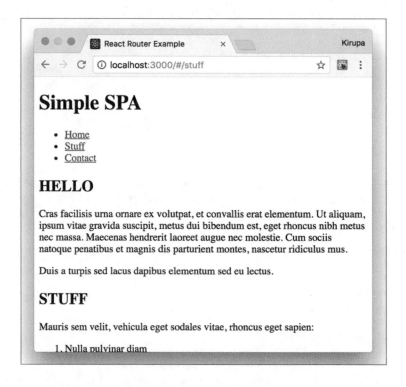

That seems problematic. We'll look at how to fix that and do many more little housekeeping tasks in the next section when we go one level deeper into using React Router.

It's the Little Things

In the previous section, we got our SPA mostly up and running. We just wrapped our entire routing region inside a `HashRouter` component, and we separated our links and the place our links load by using the `NavLink` and `Route` components, respectively. Getting our example *mostly* up and running and *fully* up and running are two different things. In the following sections, we'll close those differences.

Fixing Our Routing

We ended the previous section by determining that our routing has a bug in it. The contents of our `Home` component are always displaying because the path for loading our `Home` component is `/`. Our `Stuff` and `Contact` components have the `/` character as part of their paths as well. This means our `Home` component always matches whatever path we are trying to navigate to. The fix for that is simple. In the `Route` component representing our `Home` content, add the exact prop as shown here:

```
<div className="content">
  <Route exact path="/" component={Home}/>
  <Route path="/stuff" component={Stuff}/>
  <Route path="/contact" component={Contact}/>
</div>
```

This prop ensures that the `Route` is active only if the path is an exact match for what is being loaded. If you preview your app now, you'll see that the content loads correctly, with the `Home` content displaying only when our app is in the `Home` view.

Adding Some CSS

Right now, our app is completely unstyled. The fix for that is easy. In your `src` folder, create a file called `index.css` and add the following style rules into it:

```css
body {
  background-color: #FFCC00;
  padding: 20px;
  margin: 0;
}
h1, h2, p, ul, li {
  font-family: sans-serif;
}
```

```css
ul.header li {
  display: inline;
  list-style-type: none;
  margin: 0;
}
ul.header {
  background-color: #111;
  padding: 0;
}
ul.header li a {
  color: #FFF;
  font-weight: bold;
  text-decoration: none;
  padding: 20px;
  display: inline-block;
}
.content {
  background-color: #FFF;
  padding: 20px;
}
.content h2 {
  padding: 0;
  margin: 0;
}
.content li {
  margin-bottom: 10px;
}
```

Now, we need to reference this stylesheet in our app. At the top of index.js, add the import statement to do just that:

```javascript
import React from "react";
import ReactDOM from "react-dom";
import Main from "./Main";
import "./index.css";

ReactDOM.render(
  <Main/>,
  document.getElementById("root")
);
```

Save all your changes if you haven't done so yet. If you preview the app now, you'll notice that it's starting to look a bit more like the example we started with:

We're almost done here! We just need to do a few more things.

Highlighting the Active Link

Right now, it's hard to tell which link corresponds to content that is currently loaded. Having some sort of a visual cue would be useful. The creators of React Router have already thought of that. When you click a link, a class value of `active` is automatically assigned to it.

For example, this is what the HTML for clicking on the `Stuff` link looks like:

```
<a aria-current="true" href="#/stuff" class="active">Stuff</a>
```

All we really have to do, then, is add the appropriate CSS that lights up when an element has a class value of `active` set on it. To make this happen, go back to `index.css` and add the following style rule toward the bottom of your document:

```css
.active {
  background-color: #0099FF;
}
```

After you have added this rule and saved your document, go back to your browser and click around on the links in our example. You'll see that the active link whose content is displayed is highlighted with blue. Notice also that our Home link is always highlighted. That isn't correct. The fix is simple: Just add the `exact` prop to the `NavLink` component representing our `Home` content:

```
<li><NavLink exact to="/">Home</NavLink></li>
<li><NavLink to="/stuff">Stuff</NavLink></li>
<li><NavLink to="/contact">Contact</NavLink></li>
```

Now go back to the browser. You'll see that our Home link gets the active color treatment only when the Home content is displayed:

At this point, we're done with the code changes to build our SPA using React Router. Yay!

Conclusion

By now, we've covered a good chunk of the cool functionality React Router has in helping you build your SPA. This doesn't mean there aren't more interesting things for you to take advantage of. Our app was pretty simple, with very modest demands on the routing functionality we needed to implement. React Router provides a whole lot more (including variations of APIs for what you've seen here), so if you're building a more complex single-page app than what we've looked at so far, you should totally spend an afternoon taking a look the full React Router documentation(https://github.com/reactjs/react-router/) and examples.

> **Note: If you run into any issues, ask!**
>
> If you have any questions or your code isn't running like you expect, don't hesitate to ask! Post on the forums at https://forum.kirupa.com and get help from some of the friendliest and most knowledgeable people the Internet has ever brought together!

19

Introduction to Redux

The greatest love story of all time isn't between Romeo and Juliet. In fact, it's not even between any characters we've seen in books or movies. It's actually between React and a mysterious unknown straggler from a far-away land, known as **Redux**.

By now, you know enough about React to understand how it works and why it does some of the things it does. We haven't talked about Redux at all, though. We need to fix that before we can try to figure out why React and Redux get along so well. In the following sections, we take a deep dive into what Redux is.

What Is Redux?

If we've learned one thing in all this time, it is this: *Maintaining application state and keeping it consistent with our UI is a major challenge*. Solving this is partly why libraries such as React really took off. If you cast a wider net and look beyond just the UI layer, you'll see that maintaining application state in general is complicated. The typical app has many layers, and each layer has its own dependency on some piece of data that it relies on to do its thing.

Visualizing the relationship between your app's functionality and its application state often is pretty confusing:

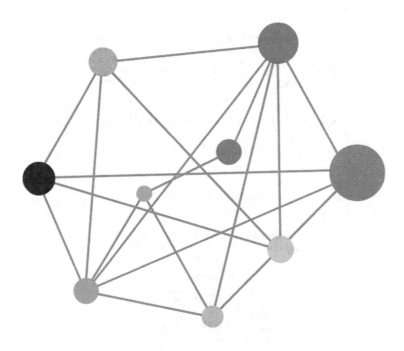

To solve this more general problem of maintaining application state, you have Redux. The easiest way to understand how Redux works is just to walk through the various pieces that go into it. The first thing we need is an app:

This app doesn't have to be anything special. It can be built in React, Angular, Vue, vanilla JS, or whatever happens to be the hot new library or framework this week. Redux doesn't care how your app is built. It only cares that your app has a magical way for dealing with application state and storing it. In the Redux world, we store **all our application state** in a single location that we'll just call the **Store**:

The thing about the Store is that reading data from it is easy. Getting information into it is a whole another story. You add a new state to (or modify existing state in) the Store by using a combination of **actions**, which describe what to change, and a **reducer**, which determines what the final state will be as a result for a given action. When you throw both of these into the picture, this is what you see:

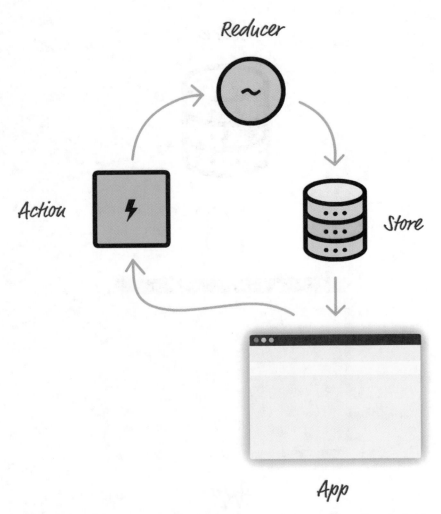

This diagram omits a few more moving pieces, but it's a good approximation of what happens when our app needs to update the state stored in the Store. Now, looking at this diagram, you're probably wondering why there's all this roundaboutness and indirection. Why can't our app just update the Store directly?

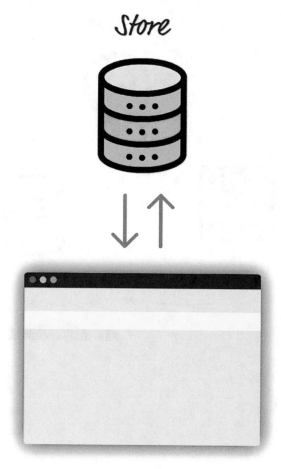

The reason is scalability. Even for simple apps, keeping our application state in-sync with what our app is doing is a chore. For complex apps in which different parts want to access and modify the application state, forget about it! This roundabout way is Redux's answer for making sure storing application state is easy for both simple apps and complex ones. Beyond just ease, Redux helps make maintaining your application state **predictable**. Dan Abramov and Andrew Clark, the creators of Redux, interpreted *predictable* as follows:

1. **Your entire application's state is stored in a single location.** You don't have to search across a variety of data stores to find the part of your state you want to update. Keeping everything stored in a single location also ensures that you don't have to worry about keeping all of this data in sync.

2. **Your state should be read-only and can be modified only through actions.** As you saw in the diagram earlier, in a Redux world, you need to ensure that random parts of your app can't access the Store and modify the state stored inside it. The only way our app can modify what is in the Store is by relying on actions.

3. **You specify what the final state should be.** To keep things simple, your state is never modified or mutated. You use a reducer to specify what the final result of your state should be.

These three principles might seem a bit abstract, but as you start to write some Redux code, you'll see them put into practice.

Building a Simple App Using Redux

We're now going to take all the diagrams and text you saw in the previous section and turn them into code. The app we're building to highlight how Redux works will be a really simple console-driven app without any UI. This app will store and display a list of favorite colors. From our app, you'll be able to add colors and remove colors. That's pretty much it.

This might seem like a step backward from the UI-rich apps we've been building, but this app will tie together all this theoretical Redux knowledge to produce some tangible lines of code. The goal is to simply make sense of Redux. We'll complicate our world by combining Redux with some UI later.

It's Redux Time

First we need to create a new HTML document and reference the Redux library as part of it. We won't be using `create-react-app` or any fancy build system here. This will be just a loose HTML file somewhere that you can view in your browser. Using your favorite code editor, go ahead and create a new file called `favoriteColors.html` and add the following markup:

```
<!DOCTYPE html>
<html>

<head>
  <title>Favorite Colors!</title>
  <script src="https://unpkg.com/redux@latest/dist/redux.js"></script>
</head>

<body>
  <script>

  </script>
</body>

</html>
```

As you can see, we have an empty HTML document with only the basic structure defined. We're referencing a hosted version of the Redux library, which is fine for kicking the tires like we're doing. For production apps, like the ones you saw with React, you have better approaches to use. We'll look at those better approaches later, but referencing the library directly is okay for now.

Lights! Camera! Action!

With our Redux library referenced, we need to define our actions. Remember, the action is the *only* mechanism we have to communicate with our Store. For our app, because we want to add and remove colors, our actions will represent that want in a way the Store will understand.

Inside your `script` tag, add the following lines:

```
function addColor(value) {
  return {
    type: "ADD",
    color: value
  };
}


function removeColor(value) {
  return {
    type: "REMOVE",
    color: value
  };
}
```

We have two functions, `addColor` and `removeColor`. They each take one argument and return an action object as a result. For `addColor`, the action object is the highlighted two lines:

```
function addColor(value) {
  return {
    type: "ADD",
    color: value
  };
}
```

When defining an action, you have a lot of freedom. Every action object has a type property. This is a keyword that signals what you're intending to do. Beyond that, any other information you send along with your action is entirely up to you. Because we're interested in adding or removing a color value from our Store, our action object also has a `color` property that stores the color we're interested in.

Let's get back to our `addColor` and `removeColor` functions. Both really serve just one purpose: to return an action. There's a more formal name for these functions in the Redux world. They're known as **action creators** because they, um, create an action.

Our Reducer

Our actions define what we want to do, but the reducer handles the specifics of what happens and how our new state is defined. You can think of the reducer as the intermediary between the Store and the outside world, where it does the following three things:

1. Provides access to the Store's original state
2. Allows you to inspect the action that was currently fired
3. Allows you to set the Store's new state

You can see all this when you add a reducer to deal with adding and removing colors from the Store. Add the following code after the point where you've defined your action creators:

```
function favoriteColors(state, action) {
  if (state === undefined) {
    state = [];
  }

  if (action.type === "ADD") {
    return state.concat(action.color);
  } else if (action.type === "REMOVE") {
    return state.filter(function(item) {
      return item !== action.color;
    });
  } else {
    return state;
  }
}
```

Take a moment to walk through what this code is doing. First we ensure that we actually have some state to fiddle with:

```
function favoriteColors(state, action) {
  if (state === undefined) {
    state = [];
  }

  if (action.type === "ADD") {
    return state.concat(action.color);
  } else if (action.type === "REMOVE") {
    return state.filter(function(item) {
      return item !== action.color;
    });
  } else {
    return state;
  }
}
```

If our state object doesn't exist, as with the first time we launch our app, we just initialize it as an empty array. You can use any data structure you want, but an array is the right one for what we're trying to do here.

From there, the rest of our code is responsible for dealing with our actions. Note that the reducer gets the full action object via its `action` argument. This means you have access to not only the action's `type` property, but also anything else you specified earlier as part of defining your actions.

For this example, if our action's type is ADD, we add the color (specified by the action's `color` property) to our state array. If our action's type is REMOVE, we return a new array with the color in question omitted. Lastly, if our action's type is something we don't know, we just return our current state, unmodified:

```
function favoriteColors(state, action) {
  if (state === undefined) {
    state = [];
  }

  if (action.type === "ADD") {
    return state.concat(action.color);
  } else if (action.type === "REMOVE") {
    return state.filter(function(item) {
      return item !== action.color;
    });
  } else {
    return state;
  }
}
```

Pretty simple, right? Be sure to keep one important Redux design choice in mind. The Redux documentation (https://redux.js.org/docs/basics/Reducers.html) describes it best:

Things you should *never* do inside a reducer:

- Mutate its arguments
- Perform side effects like API calls and routing transitions
- Call non-pure functions, e.g. `Date.now()` or `Math.random()`

Given the same arguments, it should calculate the next state and return it. No surprises. No side effects. No API calls. No mutations. Just a calculation.

You can see this in our code. To add new color values to our state array, we used the `concat` method, which returns an entirely new array made up of both the old values and the new value we're adding. Using `push` would give us the same end result, but it violates our goal of not modifying the existing state. To remove color values, we continue to maintain our goal of not modifying our current state. We use the `filter` method, which returns a brand new array with the value we want to remove omitted.

Also keep the following in mind, as Mark Erikson (@acemarke) reminded me: *Redux doesn't contain any mechanics to prevent us from modifying state and making other poor choices.* The creators of Redux have provided some guidelines. It's up to us to follow them and put those guidelines into practice.

Store Stuff

All that remains now is to tie our actions and the reducer with our Store. First we have to actually create the Store. Below your `favoriteColors` reducer function, add the following:

```
var store = Redux.createStore(favoriteColors);
```

Here we're creating a new Store using the `createStore` method. The argument we provide is the `favoriteColors` reducer we created a few moments ago. We've now come full circle in using Redux to store application state. We have our store, we have our reducer, and we have actions that tell our reducer what to do.

To see everything fully working, we're going to add (and remove) some colors to the Store. To do this, we use the `dispatch` method on our `store` object that takes an action as its argument. Go ahead and add the following lines:

```
store.dispatch(addColor("blue"));
store.dispatch(addColor("yellow"));
store.dispatch(addColor("green"));
store.dispatch(addColor("red"));
store.dispatch(addColor("gray"));
store.dispatch(addColor("orange"));
store.dispatch(removeColor("gray"));
```

Each `dispatch` call sends an action to our reducer. The reducer takes the action and performs the appropriate work to define our new state. To see the Store's current state, you can just add the following after all the `dispatch` calls:

```
console.log(store.getState());
```

As its name implies, the `getState` method returns the state's value. If you preview your app in the browser and bring up your browser's developer tools, you'll see that the colors we added get displayed in the console:

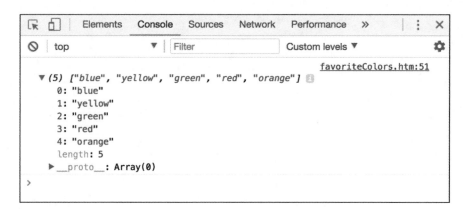

We're almost done here; We have just one more really important thing to cover. In real-world scenarios, you want to be notified each time your application's state is modified. This push model will make your life much easier if you want to update UI or perform other tasks as a result of some change to the Store. To accomplish this, you have the `subscribe` method for specifying a function (a.k.a. a listener) that gets called each time the contents of the Store are modified. To see the `subscribe` method in action, just after you defined the `store` object, add the following highlighted lines:

```
var store = Redux.createStore(favoriteColors);
store.subscribe(render);

function render() {
  console.log(store.getState());
}
```

After you've done this, preview your app again. This time, whenever you call `dispatch` to fire another action, the `render` function gets called when the Store is modified. Phew!

Conclusion

We've taken a whirlwind tour of Redux and the major pieces of functionality it brings to the table. We looked at not only the concepts that make Redux really useful for dealing with application state, but also the code to make everything real. The only thing we didn't get to do was create a more realistic example. Redux is flexible enough to work with any UI framework, and each UI framework has its own magic in working with Redux. Our UI framework of choice is, of course, React! We'll look at how to tie them together in the next chapter.

> ### Note: If you run into any issues, ask!
>
> If you have any questions or your code isn't running like you expect, don't hesitate to ask! Post on the forums at https://forum.kirupa.com and get help from some of the friendliest and most knowledgeable people the Internet has ever brought together!

20

Using Redux with React

Now that you have a better idea of how Redux works, let's look at the topic we set out to better understand in the first place. *Why is Redux so popular in React projects?* To help answer this, take a look at the following component hierarchy for some arbitrary app:

What this app does isn't very important. The only detail we'll throw in here is that some of these components are responsible for managing state and transferring some of that state around in the form of props:

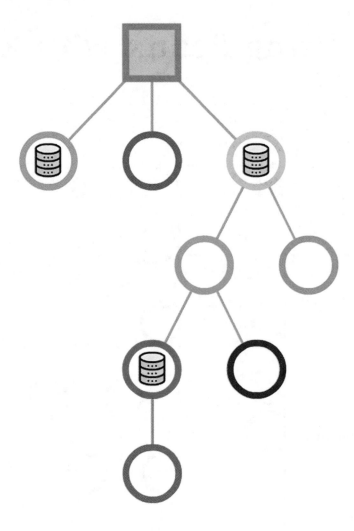

In an ideal setup, the data that each component needs flows neatly down from parent to child:

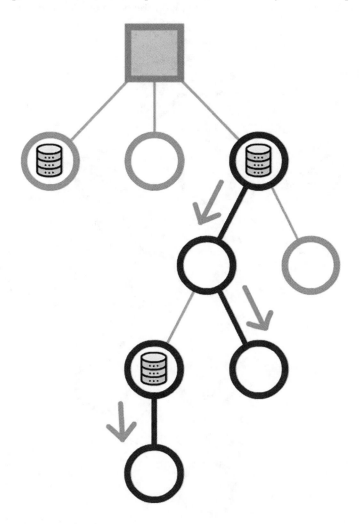

Unfortunately, outside of simple scenarios, what we want to do isn't very realistic. Your typical app does a lot of state generating, processing, and transferring. One component might initiate a state change. Another component somewhere else will want to react to it.

The props related to this state change might travel both down the tree (yay!) as well as up the tree (no!) to reach whatever component is relying on the data being transferred:

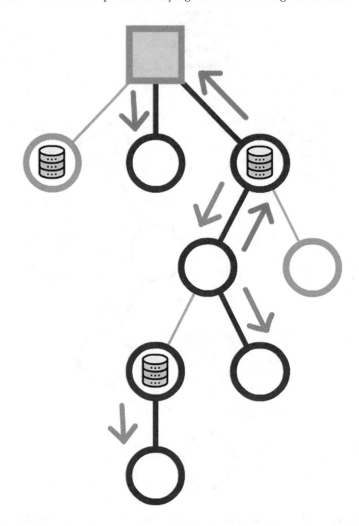

We've been guilty of this quite a few times ourselves as part of communicating something (variable value, function/event handler reference, and so on) from child to parent and beyond.

At this point, we need to acknowledge a few problems that can arise from data traveling willy nilly through our components:

1. **Dependencies make our code difficult to maintain.** React's stated goal was to avoid spaghetti-like dependencies. When we have data flowing around our app, we end up with exactly what we were supposed to be free from.

2. **Each time your state changes or a prop is transmitted, all affected components are asked to re-render.** To ensure that your UI is in sync with the current state, this behavior is a good thing. As we mentioned previously, many components are unnecessarily asked to re-render when they're simply passing a value from parent to child, with no additional input. We looked at ways of minimizing this re-rendering by setting `shouldComponentUpdate` or relying on `PureComponent`, but both approaches are a hassle to keep in sync as your app's data needs evolve.

3. **Our component hierarchy mimics the UI, not our data needs.** The way we arrange and nest our components helps separate our UI into smaller and manageable pieces. This is the correct approach. Despite the correctness, the components that initiate a state change and the ones that need to react to it are often not in the same parent/child/descendant arrangement (a.k.a. subtree). Similar to what we talked about in #ii, this requires our props to travel great distances, often multiple times per change.

The solution to our problems is Redux. Now, Redux doesn't fully solve all of these problems, but it gets us really close. Redux allows you to have all of your application's state live inside its data store instead of being distributed across a bunch of components:

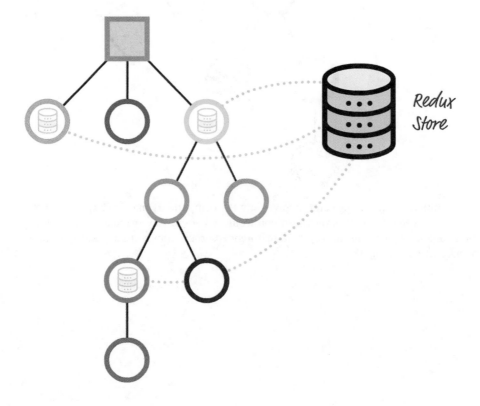

This approach solves several problems. If you want to share data from one part of your app with another, you can do that without having to navigate up and down your component hierarchy:

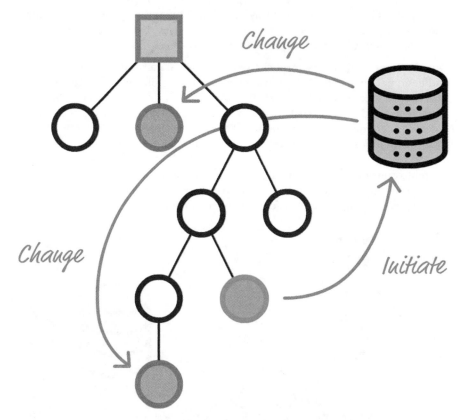

You can initiate a state change and involve only the components that are impacted directly. This directness reduces a lot of overhead you would otherwise have to maintain to ensure that your data (and any changes to it) gets to its intended destination without causing unnecessary renders. Pretty cool, right?

Now let's go one level higher. From an architectural point of view, the overview of Redux you got in the Introduction still holds:

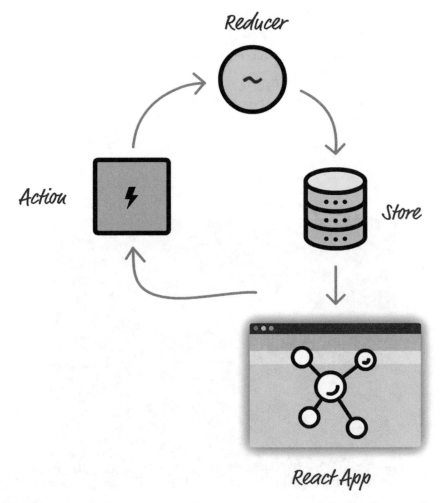

Besides the Store, we still have to work with actions, reducers, and all the other related pieces that make up the Redux party. The only difference is that our app is built using React, and this difference (and how it plays with Redux) is where we focus our attention here.

Onward!

Managing React State with Redux

The way Redux plugs into your React app is as straightforward as calling a few Redux APIs from your React code. Just two steps are involved:

1. Give your app a reference to the Redux store.

2. Map the action creators, dispatch functions, and state as props to whatever component needs data from the Store.

To see what's involved in bringing these two steps to life, we're going to build a simple Counter app that looks as in Figure 20.1:

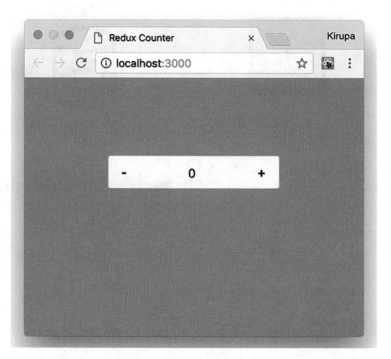

Figure 20.1   An example of the counter app we will create.

Our app will have a plus button and a minus button to increase or decrease a counter value. That's it. Nothing else is going on here; this is just the right level of functionality and complexity to help you get your feet wet with combining React and Redux.

How Redux and React Overlap

This is generally where we'd start copying and pasting HTML, CSS, and JavaScript to get our example up and running. We'll totally get there in a few moments, but first we need to walk through how this app is structured. Ignoring the data and state management side, we're going to have just two components (Figure 20.2):

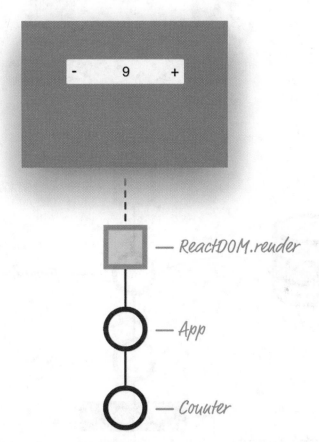

Figure 20.2   How our app is currently set up.

We'll have an App component and a Counter component. Now, a counter isn't the most complicated of examples to think about. If we had to implement it using plain old state, we would simply create a state object inside Counter and have a variable whose value increases or decreases, depending on what button we press.

When we throw Redux into the mix, our component arrangement gets a little bizarre. It will look as in Figure 20.3:

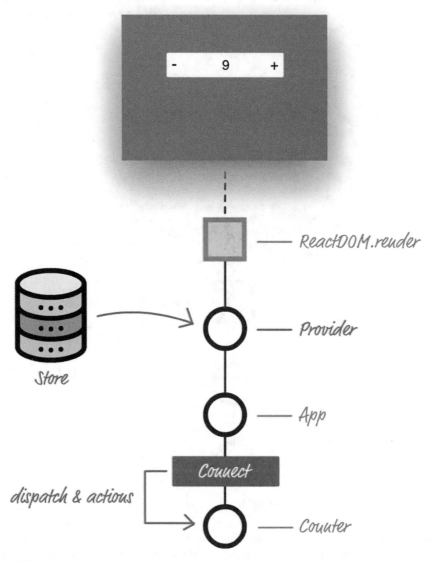

Figure 20.3   What our app's arrangement will be once we add Redux into the mix.

The items in blue are what we originally had. The items in green are new as part of incorporating Redux into our app. Earlier, we mentioned that adding Redux to our app involved two steps. The green additions mimic those steps closely:

1. The first step of providing access to our Redux store is handled by the `Provider` component.

2. The second step of granting any interested components access to our dispatch and actions is handled by the `Connect` component.

Going into a little more detail, the `Provider` component is the gateway to getting Redux functionality in our React app. It is responsible for storing a reference to the Store and ensuring that all components in our app have a way of accessing it. It is able to do that by being the topmost component in your component hierarchy. That vaulted position allows it to easily pass Redux-related wisdom throughout the entire app.

The `Connect` component is a bit more interesting. It isn't a full-blown component in the traditional sense. It's known as a Higher Order Component (https://reactjs.org/docs/higher-order-components.html), or HOC, as the cool kids say it. HOCs provide a consistent way to extend the functionality of a preexisting component by simply wrapping it and injecting their own additional functionality into it. Think of this as the React-friendly way to mimic what the `extends` keyword does when working with ES6 classes. Looking at our diagram, the end result is that, thanks to the `Connect` HOC, our `Counter` component has access to any actions and dispatch calls needed to work with the Redux Store, without you having to write any special code to access it. The `Connect` HOC takes care of that.

Both the `Provider` and `Connect` HOCs create a symbiotic relationship that gives any old React app the ability to easily work with Redux's peculiar (yet totally efficient and awesome) way of managing the application state. As we start to build our app, you'll see how this relationship plays out.

Getting Started

Now that you have an idea of how our app will be structured and some of the Redux-specific constructs we'll be using, let's shift gears and start to build our app. To get started, first use `create-react-app` to create an app we'll call `reduxcounter`:

```
create-react-app reduxcounter
```

Now let's install the Redux and React Redux dependencies. From inside your terminal/command-line environment, navigate to the `reduxcounter` folder and run the following command:

```
npm install redux
```

This installs the Redux library so that our app can use the basic building blocks Redux provides for fiddling with application state. After the Redux library has fully installed, we need to deal with one more dependency. Run the following command to bring over all the React Redux content:

```
npm install react-redux
```

When this command has run to completion, we'll have everything needed to both build our React app and use some Redux magic in it as well. It's time to start building our app!

Building the App

We first need to clear our package of all unnecessary and extraneous files. Go to your `src` and `public` folders, and delete all the contents you see in both locations. Then, create a new file called `index.html` in your `public` folder and add the following HTML into it:

```html
<!DOCTYPE html>
<html>

<head>
  <title>Redux Counter</title>
</head>

<body>
  <div id="container">

  </div>
</body>

</html>
```

The only point to note is that we have a `div` element with an `id` value of `container`.

Next, let's create the JavaScript that will be the entry point to our app. In the `src` folder, create a file called `index.js` and add the following contents into it:

```javascript
import React, { Component } from "react";
import ReactDOM from "react-dom";
import { createStore } from "redux";
import { Provider } from "react-redux";
import counter from "./reducer";
import App from "./App";
import "./index.css";

var destination = document.querySelector("#container");

// Store
var store = createStore(counter);
```

```
ReactDOM.render(
  <Provider store={store}>
    <App />
  </Provider>,
  destination
);
```

Take a moment to look at what we're doing here. We're first initializing our Redux store and using our trustworthy `createStore` method that takes a reducer at its argument. Our reducer is referenced by the `counter` variable, and if you look at our `import` statements, it is defined in a file called `reducer.js`. We'll deal with that in a few moments.

After creating our Store, we provide it as a prop to our `Provider` component. The `Provider` component is intended to be used as the outermost component in our app, to help ensure that every component has access to the Redux Store and related functionality:

```
ReactDOM.render(
  <Provider store={store}>
    <App />
  </Provider>,
  destination
);
```

Next, let's create our reducer. You already saw that our reducer is referenced by the counter variable and lives inside a file called `reducer.js`—which doesn't exist. Let's fix that by first creating a file called `reducer.js` in the `src` folder. After you have created this file, add the following JavaScript into it:

```
// Reducer
function counter(state, action) {
  if (state === undefined) {
    return { count: 0 };
  }

  var count = state.count;

  switch (action.type) {
    case "increase":
      return { count: count + 1 };
    case "decrease":
      return { count: count - 1 };
    default:
      return state;
  }
}

export default counter;
```

Our reducer is pretty simple. We have a count variable that we initialize to 0 if our state is empty. This reducer will deal with two action types: increase and decrease. If the action type is increase, we up our count value by 1. If our action type is decrease, we decrease our count value by 1 instead.

At this point, we're about halfway done building our example (Figure 20.4):

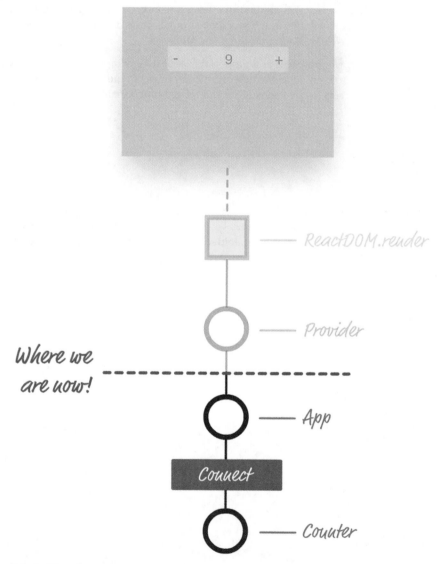

Figure 20.4 We are almost there with getting our app working!

We're ready to go one level deeper in our app and deal with our `App` component. Inside the `src` folder, create a new file called `App.js`. Inside, add the following:

```
import { connect } from "react-redux";
import Counter from "./Counter";

// Map Redux state to component props
function mapStateToProps(state) {
  return {
    countValue: state.count;
  };
}


// Action
var increaseAction = { type: "increase" };
var decreaseAction = { type: "decrease" };

// Map Redux actions to component props
function mapDispatchToProps(dispatch) {
  return {
    increaseCount: function() {
      return dispatch(increaseAction);
    },
    decreaseCount: function() {
      return dispatch(decreaseAction);
    }
  };
}

// The HOC
var connectedComponent = connect(
  mapStateToProps,
  mapDispatchToProps
)(Counter);

export default connectedComponent;
```

Take a few moments to see what's going on here. The main purpose of the code here is to turn all the Redux-specific hooks into something we can use in React. More specifically, we provide all those hooks as props that our component can easily consume through two functions, called `mapStateToProps` and `mapDispatchToProps`.

First up is our `mapStateToProps` function:

```
// Map Redux state to component props
function mapStateToProps(state) {
  return {
    countValue: state.count;
  };
}
```

This function subscribes to all Store updates and gets called when anything in our Store changes. It returns an object that contains the Store data you want to transmit as props to a component. In our case, what we're transmitting is pretty simple: an object that contains a property called countValue whose value is represented by our old count property from the Store.

Providing the Store value as props is only one part of what we need to do. The next part is to give our component access to the action creators and actions, also in the form of props. The following code handles this:

```
// Action
var increaseAction = { type: "increase" };
var decreaseAction = { type: "decrease" };

// Map Redux actions to component props
function mapDispatchToProps(dispatch) {
  return {
    increaseCount: function() {
      return dispatch(increaseAction);
    },
    decreaseCount: function() {
      return dispatch(decreaseAction);
    }
  };
}
```

The really interesting stuff happens with mapDispatchToProps. We return an object containing the name of the two functions our component can call to dispatch a change to our Store. The increaseCount function fires off a dispatch with an action type of increase. The decreaseCount function fires off a dispatch with an action type of decrease. If you look at the reducer we added a few moments ago, you can see how either of these function calls will affect the value of count we're storing in our Store.

All that remains now is to ensure that whatever component we want to provide all these props to has some way of actually receiving them. That is where the magical connect function comes in:

```
var connectedComponent = connect(
  mapStateToProps,
  mapDispatchToProps
)(Counter);
```

This function creates the magical Connect HOC we talked about earlier. It takes our mapStateToProps and mapDispatchToProps functions as arguments, and it passes all of that into the Counter component, which you also specify. The end result of all this code running is the equivalent of rendering the following:

```
<Connect>
  <Counter increaseCount={increaseCount}
           decreaseCount={decreaseCount}
           countValue={countValue}/>
</Connect>
```

Our `Counter` component gets access to `increaseCount`, `decreaseCount`, and `countValue`. The only strange thing is that there's no `render` function or equivalent in sight. All of that is handled automatically by React and its treatment of HOC.

We're almost done! It's time to get our `Counter` component up and running. In your `src` directory, add a file called `Counter.js`. Put the following into it:

```
import React, { Component } from "react";

class Counter extends Component {
  render() {
    return (
      <div className="container">
        <button className="buttons"
                onClick={this.props.decreaseCount}>-</button>
        <span>{this.props.countValue}</span>
        <button className="buttons"
                onClick={this.props.increaseCount}>+</button>
      </div>
    );
  }
}


export default Counter;
```

This will probably be the most boring component you've seen in quite some time. We've already talked about how our `Connect` HOC sends down props and other related shenanigans to our `Counter` component. You can see those props in use here to display the `counter` value or call the appropriate function when our plus or minus buttons are clicked.

The last thing we need to do is define our CSS file to style our counter. In the same `src` folder we've been working in all this time, create a file called `index.css`. Inside this file, add the following style rules:

```
body {
  margin: 0;
  padding: 0;
  font-family: sans-serif;
  display: flex;
  justify-content: center;
  background-color: #8E7C93;
}

.container {
  background-color: #FFF;
  margin: 100px;
  padding: 10px;
  border-radius: 3px;
  width: 200px;
```

```css
  display: flex;
  align-items: center;
  justify-content: space-between;
}

.buttons {
  background-color: transparent;
  border: none;
  font-size: 16px;
  font-weight: bold;
  border-radius: 3px;
  transition: all .15s ease-in;
}

.buttons:hover:nth-child(1) {
  background-color: #F45B69;
}

.buttons:hover:nth-child(3) {
  background-color: #C0DFA1;
}
```

At this point, we're done with our example. If you haven't done so yet, save your changes across all the files you've been working on. If you preview your app in the browser (using npm start), you will see your counter working as expected.

Conclusion

In many ways, Redux is designed to fix some of the shortcomings that React often claims as advantages. We looked at some of these advantages when we examined how data in React is supposed to flow. You could even go further and say that the ideas behind Redux should be formalized as part of React itself so that you get even better integration. But Redux isn't perfect, either. As with many things in programming, Redux is simply one of many tools you have for accomplishing a task. Not every situation involving data requires Redux; in fact, adding Redux sometimes can create unnecessary complexity in what you're trying to do. Dan Abramov, one of the creators of Redux, wrote a great article (https://medium.com/@dan_abramov/you-might-not-need-redux-be46360cf367) describing some situations when you probably shouldn't use Redux to solve your problem. I highly encourage you to read that to get the full picture.

> ### Note: If you run into any issues, ask!
>
> If you have any questions or your code isn't running like you expect, don't hesitate to ask! Post on the forums at https://forum.kirupa.com and get help from some of the friendliest and most knowledgeable people the Internet has ever brought together!

Index

B

S

T

U

V

W-X-Y-Z

REGISTER YOUR PRODUCT at informit.com/register

Access Additional Benefits and SAVE 35% on Your Next Purchase

- Download available product updates.

- Access bonus material when applicable.

- Receive exclusive offers on new editions and related products.
  (Just check the box to hear from us when setting up your account.)

- Get a coupon for 35% for your next purchase, valid for 30 days. Your code will
  be available in your InformIT cart. (You will also find it in the Manage Codes
  section of your account page.)

Registration benefits vary by product. Benefits will be listed on your account page
under Registered Products.

InformIT.com–The Trusted Technology Learning Source

InformIT is the online home of information technology brands at Pearson, the world's foremost
education company. At InformIT.com you can

- Shop our books, eBooks, software, and video training.
- Take advantage of our special offers and promotions (informit.com/promotions).
- Sign up for special offers and content newsletters (informit.com/newsletters).
- Read free articles and blogs by information technology experts.
- Access thousands of free chapters and video lessons.

Connect with InformIT–Visit informit.com/community

Learn about InformIT community events and programs.

the trusted technology learning source

Addison-Wesley · Cisco Press · IBM Press · Microsoft Press · Pearson IT Certification · Prentice Hall · Que · Sams · VMware Press

Accessing the Free Web Edition

Your purchase of this book in any format includes access to the corresponding
Web Edition, which provides several special online-only features:

- The complete text of the book

- Updates and corrections as they become available

The Web Edition can be viewed on all types of computers and mobile devices with
any modern web browser that supports HTML5.

To get access to the *Learning React* Web Edition, all you need to do is register
this book:

1. Go to www.informit.com/register.

2. Sign in or create a new account.

3. Enter the ISBN: **9780134843551**.

4. Answer the questions as proof of purchase.

5. The Web Edition will appear under the Digital Purchases tab on your
   Account page. Click the Launch link to access the product.